When the Boomers Bail

A Community Economic Survival Guide

By Mark Lautman

ISBN 978-0-9817869-3-3

Library of Congress Control Number: 2010932543

Graphics by Kevin Brown and Megan Cardwell
Graphics Editor: Kyrsten Sanderson
Cover by Steve Wedeen

LOGAN SQUARE PRESS
ALBUQUERQUE, NM
U.S.A.

Dedication

To my wife Mary Anne: I promise I will someday remove the white board from the living room and be somewhat normal.

And to our children Sarah, Megan and Lucas: If we had known that making you talk to me about economic development would have been so emotionally scarring, we would have used corporal punishment instead.

Thank you all for everything. You have made my life.

Acknowledgements

This book is the result of thousands of hours of collaboration, critical thinking and encouragement by almost everyone I know. But I want to acknowledge some of the people who played critical roles in the process.

Family

No one bore a greater burden or made a bigger contribution than my wife Mary Anne. She understood from the beginning that I needed to be an economic developer to be happy. The depth and duration of her love and support goes way beyond anything I ever expected or deserved. My three kids, Sarah, Megan and Lucas, were subjected to so much talk about economic development that they came to call it the E-word. I'm grateful for both their indulgence and their contributions of insight and logic during the writing process.

I also need to acknowledge my parents and grandparents for cultivating a family ethos for making the world a better place.

Friends and Colleagues

In the end, it was three of my closest friends, Bill Knauf, Jeff Spiegel, and Dale Dekker who kept the pressure on me to finish. I also want to acknowledge many of my colleagues and friends who collaborated, corroborated and encouraged the development of the ideas and convictions expressed in the book: Ron Smith, Kevin Reid, Noreen Scott, Tracy Leonard, James Jimenez, Art Corsie, Will Hearn, Tim Nitti, Mike Hickey, Jim Covell, Dr. Brian McDonald, Dr. Jim Peach, Brian Sanderoff, Dr. Garrey Carruthers, Dr. Vipin Gupta, Dr. Kelly O'Donnell, Jim Kinnett, Jack Allston, Jim Glover, Bill and

Laurie Moye, Barry Lang, Gerry Wendell, Albert Ratner and Paul Martini, Charles Tafoya, Dr. Charles Grantham, Dr. James Ware, Joan Laurence, Mark Mathis, Steve McKee and Rodger Beimer. Each provided critical analysis, insight and inspiration during the process.

Thought Leaders

My thinking on the subject matter in this book has been shaped by the works of a long list of thought leaders, including Ken Dychtwald, Tamara Ericson, Richard Florida, Malcolm Gladwell, Daniel Pink, Lou Tice, Manji Inoue, Peter Calthorpe, Gerald Yonas, Joel Kotkin, Thomas Friedman, Warren Bennis, Eliseo Carrasco, Kurt Gottleib, Laurence Kotlicoff, Scott Burns, Jane Jacobs, and Ralph Waldo Emerson.

My Writing Team

Being neither a scholar nor a writer, I required a substantial level of collaboration, coaching and editing support. Early in the process I was urged on by friends Mark Mathis and Steve McKee, who were in the process of writing and publishing their own books.

In 2006 and 2007, I worked with a gifted and intellectually engaging writer named Cory Williamson in what turned out to be more of a ghostwriting role. As the 2008 recession unfolded, the emerging manuscript entitled *Catastrophic Full Employment* was losing relevance and urgency, and we decided to shelve the project.

Although very little of the work we did on that manuscript made it into this book, it was incredibly constructive. I count Cory and his wife Maria among my closest friends.

After a casual conversation in 2009 with a local Albuquerque writer Dennis Domrzalski about my epiphany that economic development as we know it and practice it is probably over in most places, he encouraged me to take a few months off and try to kick out a manuscript by writing from a stream of consciousness. He agreed to look in on me a couple of times a month, coach me and be my editor. If you find the book valuable and readable, it is due in large part to Dennis' encouragement, good humor, insight, instincts and editing skills. I also want to thank Roxanne Blair, a family friend and recent Notre Dame grad, and Evan Karr, now a student at Georgetown University, who helped me clarify concepts, do research, check facts and polish the prose. Kevin Brown provided graphic design.

I need to thank my friends and colleagues in the Community Economics Lab who invested the time to read and critique the early drafts. I am grateful. Your comments dramatically improved the end product.

Contents

Introduction

In 2005, I had an epiphany that scared the hell out of me. It would change the way I looked at everything I care about—my kids, my professional career, my financial security, my community and my country. Almost sixty years old and at the top of my profession, the last thing I needed or expected was to have to confront a new reality, one that would force me to question my basic outlook on life, my political philosophy and the value of my vocation.

I thought, "We're screwed." I discovered a problem bigger than climate change, Islamic terrorism, the collapse of the global financial system and the rest of the top ten things the world is worried about. And this one is not even on our radar screens. It's imminent and irreversible, and it is going to wreck the quality of our lives, the companies we work for, the communities we live in and our country way before New Yorkers have to buy their first pair of waders. If you are worried about any of those problems, you should worry about this one first because it is going to rob us of the resources needed to deal with any of them.

The problem—actually there are four of them—is simple. We Baby Boomers didn't have enough kids, our birth rate isn't high enough, we're living longer, and our educational system is dropping half our kids in the academic dirt. As 78 million of us retire, there won't be enough qualified workers behind us to fill the jobs and grow the economy that's necessary to support all us new dependents.

Communities and companies will fight each other for jobs and qualified workers. Some communities will win and prosper. Others will fail. Those that fail will be a mess. There won't be enough qualified workers to fill demanding jobs. Businesses will not only not come to those communities, they will leave them. That will shrink tax bases and revenues that support many of the public institutions we all depend on. Roads, sewer and water systems will go unrepaired. Public hospitals will be pinched, and more and more people will go untreated. Store fronts will be boarded up and main streets will look like a mouth missing too many teeth. School systems will have to cut back, and the educational system will deteriorate even further.

If you're stuck in one of those failing communities and want to leave, you might not be able to. You won't be able to sell your house because there won't be anyone to buy it. If you don't have the education, skills and experience needed by the market, you'll be stuck—in more ways than one. You probably won't be able to sell your business either. It'll be a mess. But if you're prepared, know the warning signs and act, you might be able to avoid it all.

The biggest problem we're facing is *full employment.*

It's imminent, will be catastrophic and our biggest national security problem. I know it sounds crazy. With more than 14 million of our countrymen out of work, how could full employment be our biggest problem?

The cause of it all is that we Baby Boomers didn't have enough kids to replace ourselves, we didn't properly educate the few we did have, and we're living longer, which means that when we start to retire, we are going to run out of the qualified workers needed to staff the economy—an economy that will need to grow to keep pace with a still-growing population.

Why will this be catastrophic? Because our population is growing on the dependent side—the old, the sick and those who lack the education and skills to earn more than they need to live on. The proportion of the population that produces more than they consume will shrink until it's too small to support the economy.

What will happen when we reach full employment? How will we create the new jobs needed to generate the extra tax revenue to pay for the swelling ranks of dependents? The reality is that in most communities we won't. At this point, economic development as we know it will be over.

Here's the catastrophic part: Community economies need to grow a little faster than their populations in order for families, companies, their tax-dependent institutions and the country to improve and prosper. When an economy grows slower than the population it has to serve, there will be more people every year and fewer and fewer resources to support them. It gets ugly. When the economy grows slower than the population for an extended period of time, it becomes a catastrophe.

In the past, economic contractions were short and mostly caused by the excesses of the business cycle. This time the problem is being caused by structural demographic conditions that will get steadily worse for the next two decades. Every person you will hire in the next twenty-five years has already been born. So it's too late for those of us who caused this problem to go back and fix the school system and have two or three more kids.

We are heading into a twenty-five-year, zero-sum labor market where all the qualified workers in your community will have a job—or two if they want. If your community isn't producing enough qualified new workers—and most aren't even close—and you are not in one of those cool, hip places that attract talented workers, then you will be out of headroom to grow your economy. The day you hit full employment is the day you are out of the economic development business. Your community managers will have no levers left to push to make ends meet. Your community will enter an economic death spiral that will last the rest of our lifetime.

Without enough qualified workers to go around, one community's gain will be another one's loss. One company's gain will come at the expense of a competitor. Economic development won't be a game that everyone can win at anymore. Some will have to lose. It won't be equitable. It won't be fair. It will turn into a demographic civil war.

This is going to happen in thousands of communities across the U.S., Canada and the rest of the industrialized world in the next decade. Not only is it the end of economic development as we know and practice it today, it is probably the biggest national security threat we have ever faced. If we can't staff a superpower economy, we won't be able to afford the military or the commercial and social programs that keep us safe and make the world a better place.

How you, your family and your employer do in this frightening scenario will depend a lot on where you live and how well your community is managed and positioned. The focus of this book is how catastrophic full employment threatens the solvency of our hometowns, who the winners and losers will be, and what, if anything, you can do about it.

Right now, community leaders are understandably preoccupied with trying to balance budgets as revenues shrink. Meanwhile, the internet is changing how we do business, how we work and why we live and work where we do. Concerns about climate change and economic security are permanently altering consumption patterns. Excessive public and private debt threaten to starve our economies of the capital they need to automate and grow.

Our leaders are oblivious and completely unprepared for what is coming next—the mother of all economic threats.

I came to this epiphany slowly and reluctantly. In late 2005 I was working for a large national development company that had won the right to develop one of the largest tracts of undeveloped urban land in the country. At build-out in thirty-five to fifty years, it would be home to 100,000 new residents, in effect, a new city within a city. As the economic architect for the project, my job was to figure out what kind of economy could be developed to support the new community and execute an economic development program that guaranteed the people of Albuquerque that we would not be building the project on the backs of existing taxpayers.

Our winning bid included a commitment to create twice as many new economic base jobs—jobs that export goods and services and import wealth—on the site than we would need to support the new residential population. We would have to create these new jobs proportionally out ahead of the new housing or we would be denied further building permits or tax increment financing. As far as we could tell, we were the first developer in the country to commit to a hard number threshold for new jobs as a formal condition for building and selling homes.

After winning the bid, we had a short time to finalize development agreements with the city and get final corporate approval to write a big check and go hard on hundreds of millions of dollars of new infrastructure bonds. The evening before the big "go or no go" board meeting, Albert Ratner, chairman of Forest City Enterprises, an $11 billion publicly-traded-company, asked me, "Is there anything keeping you up at night about our ability to meet these job-creation metrics? You know if we can't, it will doom the project and could put the company in trouble."

I told him there was. Our final development agreement called for creation of 30,000 net new economic base jobs paying $45-50,000 a year over the life of the project. We needed to generate roughly 400 net new economic base jobs a year on the site every year for the next forty-five years or the project would fail. I knew someone from corporate was going to challenge the logic and the feasibility of our jobs-before-housing commitment. How were they likely to come at me?

The year we were hatching this brilliant economic development strategy and selling it to the company and local government officials, Albuquerque's unemployment rate dropped steadily from 3.8 percent to 3.6, to 3.5, to a bottom of 3.3 percent. At that rate, unemployment would be 2.8 percent by the time we were scheduled to build the first house in 2008. How would we be able to get employers to come to Albuquerque to create 400 new jobs every year on our site if there weren't any qualified workers available in the market? The obvious answer was that we wouldn't. The rebuttal to that was that companies would come from other states. The next questions: Would they really? And where would they come from?

A few weeks before I had come across a graph in Ken Dychtwald and Tamara Ericson's book *Workforce Crisis* that made my heart stop. It was the Inverted Labor Supply Curve. It showed the U.S. running short of the labor needed to fill jobs in demand sometime in 2008, and that the gap would widen steadily for the next twenty-plus years. The year 2008 just happened to be the year our housing program was to begin. It was a coincidence that we were going to start a thirty-year-long development project in which we would have to create twice the number of jobs we needed, in the same year and on the exact date the national labor market was predicted to go upside down—and it was going to get worse every year we were in business.

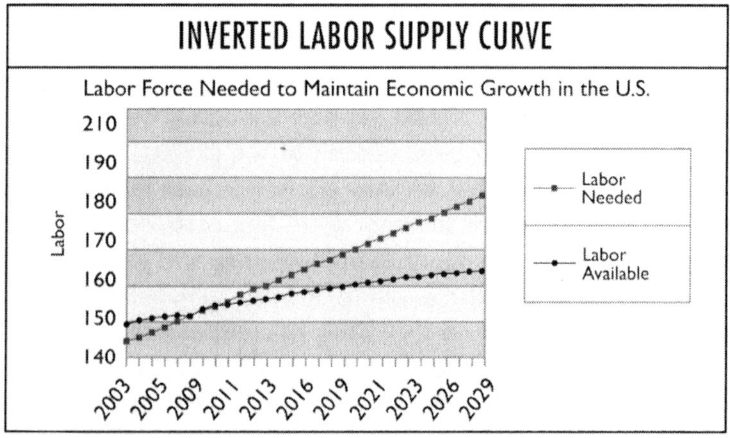

I first thought that the graph was mislabeled. The whole country is going to run out of labor, I thought to myself? Actually, the entire industrialized world is! After *Workforce Crisis,* I read *The Coming Generational Storm* by Laurence Kotlikoff and Scott Burns. Barring an act of God or a complete collapse of the world economy, we were going to run out of the labor needed to grow the economy—anywhere.

What had I done? We had already committed in the development agreements that we would create these jobs. I was screwed. The company was screwed, so was the city for that matter. It was later that I realized this could mean the end of the economic development business. There I was—my world along with my role in it was blown away by a single overlooked fact: We Boomers didn't have enough offspring to replace ourselves. Some epitaph for the generation that invented "free love."

But why was I finding out about this now? Like a second semester college freshman, I was scrambling to construct a new worldview that would allow me to regain some of my professional self-confidence without admitting I was an idiot who had just doomed our company. Luckily, the "go or no go" meeting the next day went really long and I was spared the kind of grilling my fellow VPs got.

Over the next two years with an aggressive governor, a billion dollar state budget surplus and some blind luck, we recruited eight major new companies to the project. That put us ten-to-twelve years ahead of our job-creation threshold. We weren't even scheduled to start building houses for another year. I couldn't believe it. We looked like geniuses. But even then I couldn't shake the feeling of dread that the Inverted Labor Supply Curve gave me.

I felt a little like the seismologist who first saw the needle move indicating a big chunk of the floor of the Indian Ocean had given way, sending a tsunami heading toward Indonesia at five hundred miles an hour. He must have known that the warning he was sending out would come too late for many and would be ignored by others. Those heeding the warning could run for high ground and might save themselves. Others would turn and run when they saw the water pull away from the beach and form into an unnaturally giant wave.

And then there were the people like the poor bastard in the film clip that CNN aired a thousand times, standing there a hundred meters out in what was moments before waist deep water. Mesmerized by how the tide could go out so fast, and staring at the wave bringing the water back in, he never moved or even turned away as the wave crashed over him.

The seismic event that triggered the coming labor shortage happened twenty-five years ago. It's on its way. You can't stop it. Some will escape unhurt, but everyone will be affected. The record unemployment of the recent Great Recession makes the prospect of full employment hard to believe.

As a community leader you don't want to be that guy standing in the middle of an empty beach watching the tide pulled out two miles in two minutes, staring mesmerized at the wave until it's too late.

Every time I thought I found a flaw in the new paradigm, a mitigating factor, or a way to rationalize or sub-optimize it, it only illustrated another way of how this new reality would change things. For a long time I couldn't believe it—didn't want to believe it. The only thing that gave me any comfort was that no one else around me had seen it coming or could appreciate its destructive nature.

We have accepted on blind faith that a perpetually expanding economic pie means that an individual's initiative and achievement not only does not come at the expense of someone else, but actually creates an evergreen supply of new opportunities for others. It's ironic when you think about it. The Holy Grail of modern society, full employment, is now our biggest threat.

This uniquely American outlook on life, liberty and the pursuit of happiness that we have taken for granted for two hundred years is about to be tested. When it dawns on the average guy that we are sharing a shrinking pie, things will get tough.

A zero-sum labor market will create two classes of communities—winners and losers. It's going to get ugly for a lot of people and a lot of places. This book is about how the Inverted Labor Supply Curve threatens your community, and specifically, how it changes the game for the people managing our cities, counties, public schools, hospitals and public institutions.

The first part of the book will try to convince you that we are indeed looking at a catastrophic shortage of qualified labor by laying out the four underlying causes of the problem, the seven major forces at work that may alleviate it, and the thirteen that will make it worse. The second section deals with the nature of communities and why they will be even more important to our health and happiness in the future. We will also go into how local economies really work and how chronic labor shortages can send them into a death spiral.

The next section explains how to tell if the community you are living in is going to be a winner or a loser. The last section discusses some of the things communities might be able to do to deal with catastrophic full employment.

Managing our communities is a whole new game now. The stakes just went up, and it just got a lot harder. Most of us have no idea what's in store. I want this book to change the way you think. If enough people understand the gravity of the situation, community dialogue will change. Only then will priorities change and solutions come.

Mark Lautman,
Albuquerque, New Mexico

Part One

I See Old People

OPERATIONAL DEFINITION OF ECONOMIC DEVELOPMENT

E>P

E = Economy | P = Population

Chapter 1

The Temple of Doom

I see old people, and they scare me.

It's not that I'm a geezerphobe. Hell, I'm nearing geezerhood myself. It's what all us old people are going to do to our economies, our communities, and, in the end, our national security.

I see tens of millions of old people, all retired, all collecting Social Security and using Medicare benefits.

What really worries me is what I don't see: young people. That is, enough young people with the education, skills and experience to replace the 78 million Boomers as we get too slow, sick and tired to work. It's a problem that threatens the future of every community in the U.S. and most of the industrialized world.

There are actually four big irreversible forces that have created the problem. I call them the Big Four: a falling birth rate, failure to properly educate the incoming generations, rising life expectancy and the Boomer anomaly.

The Falling Birth Rate

We Baby Boomers are the first generation in history that failed to have enough children to replace ourselves. And the children of Boomers don't look like they are going to do any better. This is the big one. My parents' generation, my grandparents' generation and the generations before them had four-to-twelve kids per couple, dropping way more new workers on the doorstep of the economy every year than the existing economy needed.

This chronic imbalance of extra citizens that needed work made the unemployment rate the most important measure of a community's health and gave rise to the field of economic development. If a community's economy could not grow fast enough to employ the people who needed to work, it created a drag on the community's ability to grow and improve.

In 2008, we entered an unprecedented era where the economy will still continue to need to grow to serve a growing population, but it will now be constrained by a growing shortage of new, qualified workers. As we retire, there simply won't be enough younger workers to take our places. The problem is not unique to the U.S.; it's even worse in Europe, Japan, Russia and China.

Increasing Life Expectancy

If the populations of our communities were going to shrink in proportion to the smaller workforce, then this would not be such a big deal. But that is not going to happen.

Two factors are propelling the population and the economy to continue growing for the next twenty-five years: steadily increasing life expectancy and the demographic anomaly called the Baby Boomers. A community where the workforce is shrinking in proportion to the total population spells big trouble.

For the last one hundred years, every generation has lived longer than their parents. This might seem like a good thing. After all, who doesn't want to live longer? But it's actually bad news in this case. While the population of our country and most of our communities will continue to grow, our local economies will need to expand to serve the additional residents, especially in economic sectors driven by elders—like health care.

Despite a negative birth rate, the population will continue to grow—mostly on the old end. For the next several decades at least, instead of the workforce growing faster and coming in better educated than the older half of the population, the numbers of young, qualified workers entering the economy will be a shrinking minority of the population.

An increasingly disproportionate share of the population will be either too old to work or unable to do the jobs in demand. We are going to be loading up our communities with more and more people who consume the most expensive government services at the same time we reduce the number who produce.

The Boomer Mass Exodus

What makes these forces even harder to contend with is the physics of the demographic anomaly called the Baby Boomers. People born between 1946 and 1964 represent a huge proportion of the workforce.

The fact that so many Boomers are going to leave the workforce and become dependents so fast will be a major aspect of the problem. The fact that they are the most productive, experienced and hardest working part of the labor force is potentially catastrophic.

In demographic terms, all 78 million of us are going to disappear at once, leaving the economy without the skills, experience and knowledge to maintain current levels of production and services—not to mention to staff an economy that continues to need to expand.

In short, you have to deal with 78 million Boomers who will switch almost overnight from being producers to being dependents.

Failure to Educate the Incoming Generation of Workers

On top of not having enough children, it looks like we will have the distinction of being the first American generation to break the tradition of bringing our children up better prepared than the generation before. The U.S. public education system, once the pride of the world, is now the Achilles heel of almost every community and is becoming a national humiliation. There are some communities today that fail to get even half of their high school kids to graduate.

The dropout rate isn't the only problem. The educational bar for the jobs in the economy today, not to mention a few years from now, is being raised every year, even in rudimentary service jobs. Technology is progressing much faster than curriculums and educational standards, leaving those who do graduate increasingly unprepared for the jobs ahead.

Even if we had had enough kids to replace ourselves, the fact that we are dropping half our kids in the educational dirt means we still wouldn't have enough qualified workers to sustain our economy in the future. So we are not just in trouble because we will lack the bodies to replace ourselves in the workforce. We are going to have even fewer minds.

A Zero-Sum Game with Only Winners and Losers

Taken together, these four forces—the birth rate, life expectancy, mass exodus of Boomers and failing schools will create zero-sum labor market labor conditions for an economy that will need to continue growing. Since talent and investment are not evenly distributed across the communities in the U.S., some will fare better than others.

What a zero-sum national labor market means is there will be two classes of communities going forward: winners and losers. It means that some communities will have the educated workers they need to grow their economies and support all those dependents, and others won't.

We are talking about a demographic civil war because communities will start trying to steal each other's educated and skilled workers. When we had a chronic oversupply of workers, every community and every employer could win. Not anymore.

As we come out of this recession, most communities will reach full employment much faster than anyone expects. That means that anyone who is educated, trained, and willing and able to work will have a job. Most of the best jobs from then on will go unfilled. There will still be hordes of people without the education, training, communication skills and attitude preparation needed to qualify for and hold the jobs in demand.

The competition for the unskilled jobs will intensify as a chronic and growing oversupply of unskilled, inexperienced and unprepared workers keeps wages depressed and unemployment high. The growing ranks of those who come to the workforce unprepared to learn or earn, combined with those who have not retrained from obsolete skills, will keep unemployment rates high in many communities. That will perpetuate the myth that all you have to do is create new jobs to reduce poverty, raise household incomes and the additional discretionary tax revenue needed to make things better.

The brutal essence of this dilemma for community leaders and managers of tax-dependent institutions is that as communities reach full employment of their qualified workforce, they will suddenly be out of headroom to grow the economy.

If you run out of extra workers, you can't create new jobs to grow the economy. The day that happens you will be out of the economic development business—trapped without a way to grow.

The demands of a rapidly aging, increasingly dependent and rapidly growing population will outrun the ability of the economy to create the new jobs and the additional tax revenue needed to maintain essential services. Service and maintenance burdens of local governments and your community's tax-dependent institutions will explode while the economy that produces all the tax revenue contracts or stagnates: your basic shrinking pie.

The Collapsing Room in the Temple of Doom

The real purpose of this chapter is to scare the hell out of you. The purpose of the next chapter is to keep you from rationalizing the problem away. I want your eyes to dilate, and your heart rate and blood pressure to rise and adrenaline to start flowing when you see this graph.

Most community leaders, city managers and economic developers are hard-core optimists. It's difficult to scare people who have an optimistic outlook on life, but it is especially hard to scare them by holding up a graph called the Inverted Labor Supply Curve. We are hard-wired to respond to physical threats like running into two big menacing guys late at night in a dark parking lot in a bad part of town, or when someone threatens a loved one. But we're not hard-wired to jump into survival mode when we see an Inverted Labor Supply Curve.

There are plenty of data, reports and books available predicting the looming labor supply problem at the national level. The problem is that there is virtually no predictive data available at the regional or local level that shows the depth of the gaps between the jobs that will be in demand and the supply of qualified workers.

You can't see the statistical dimensions of the problem at the local level because the data either isn't being collected, or it's hard to get, and no one wants to make projections. The last thing politicians, community managers and school officials want to do is spend precious discretionary resources proving there is another Big Problem out there for which they have no solutions.

It just makes them look bad. Before the recession, this issue was beginning to get some attention in Canada, Australia and Europe. A handful of American governors had begun to talk about it. But it's hard to make the case that the lack of workers is our biggest problem when there are 14 million of our fellow citizens out of work.

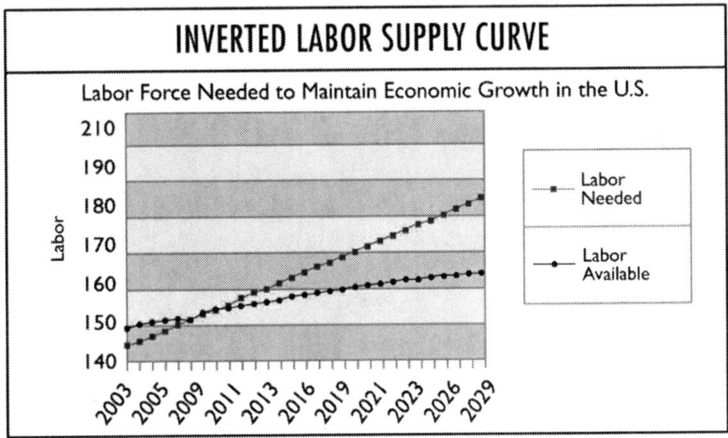

I realize that it is going to be hard to scare people with the Inverted Labor Supply Curve, but I'm going to try. Frankly, if our local leaders and others who understand how local economies work fail to recognize the inevitability and the potentially catastrophic consequences of this dilemma, we won't be able to get in front of it in time to do anything about it. It will be too late.

Think of it as if your home town is trapped in a big underground room like the one in the movie *Indiana Jones and the Temple of Doom.* Two of the opposing walls begin moving in, slowly at first, each driven by kinetic forces put into motion generations ago. The floor and ceiling are converging too.

At first, no one notices that the room is closing in. The first time someone does, they are ignored. It's happening so slowly that no one cares. When a few more notice that the walls are moving in, arguments break out about taking or delaying action. Eventually you get to the tipping point where leaders who have waited too long to lead and do anything about the converging walls are replaced, and the new ones have to deal with panic levels of concern and despair.

Today, every community is a room with moving walls. But they're not all alike. There are a few communities where the walls will move slowly and eventually stop. The walls could even start to move out—eventually letting in the sun and permitting people to come and go at their leisure.

There are many more of the second type of communities; those where the walls, floor and ceiling not only continue to converge, but accelerate to a predictable catastrophic end. You can only imagine what they are going to go through. The claustrophobic panic followed by the pain of—you get the picture. It's bad. Scared yet?

You might be lucky and be living in a community on the bubble where the occupants actually have the tools to save themselves. If community leaders can do some quick thinking, figure out the problem and how to measure it, they might be able to muster the right combination of leadership, ingenuity, cooperation and volition they'll need to stop the convergence of the walls, ceiling and floor, and maybe even reverse the process.

Which kind of room is your community in? Since most of us won't know for a while, getting to work on the problem as if you are in such a room might do some good and keep everyone positive until your fate becomes obvious. If you live in a place where action could save you, you have no time to waste.

Trying to move to another city or town could be an option. But how do you know if it's better or worse than the one you're in? If you are a community leader, aspire to be one, or just want to know if it's worth staying around—you will want to understand as much as you can about these forces and factors working on your community's economy.

In addition to the four primary forces converging on your community, there are two other lists of factors that deserve scrutiny: those that may improve the situation (mitigating), and those that are making things worse (aggravating). How your community leaders and neighbors respond will be the difference between survival and death for many communities.

Demographics is Destiny - Economics is Fiction

Demographic projections are very different from economic projections in one important way. Every person you will hire in the next twenty-five years has already been born, and we know who they are, who their parents are, how much money their family earned, how far they made it through school, and a lot of other things we probably wish we didn't know. Soon we may even know your genetic future.

My point is that the only numbers you can really count on when calculating the future is how many kids we had, how many of them got educated, and how long we are going to live. How much we might consume, the next major war, how long we will really need or value gold, how long China will continue buying U.S. Treasury notes, or how much money our government will print, is conjecture and subject to Adam Smith's invisible hand and the fickle winds of change in a complex system driven by a gazzillion variables.

Let's look at some basic population data from the U.S. Census Bureau. It may be the only data you can actually rely on these days. Thanks to our Founding Fathers, we have a reasonably trustworthy history of our population from the time of our country's birth.

The reason for their interest in this count was simple: ours is a representative democracy, and each state's representation in the House of Representatives is determined according to its population. That's why census results are so hotly contested. Leave some citizens out of the count, or include some that don't belong, and the makeup of our government changes, leaving some states overrepresented and others with fewer than their fair share of representatives.

So to start, let's take a look at the growth of the U.S. population over the past two centuries. The graph below illustrates just how steady our population growth has been, despite a succession of wars, changing rates of immigration, and the rapid expansion of our territory.

So America is still growing, and that's good news. The bad news is that's about the only good news there is.

As steady as the growth in our population has been over the last two centuries, our *rate of growth* has dropped steadily since 1900. In the nineteenth century, our country's population grew by about thirty percent every ten years. In the first half of the twentieth century, the rate of growth fell to about twenty percent every ten years, and in every decade that followed—with short-lived exceptions in the 1950s, 1970s and 1990s—the rate continued to fall until it finally reached the single-digit growth of the 1990 census. While we can only guess why the rate of growth in our population has steadily declined, we can easily demonstrate how it happened.

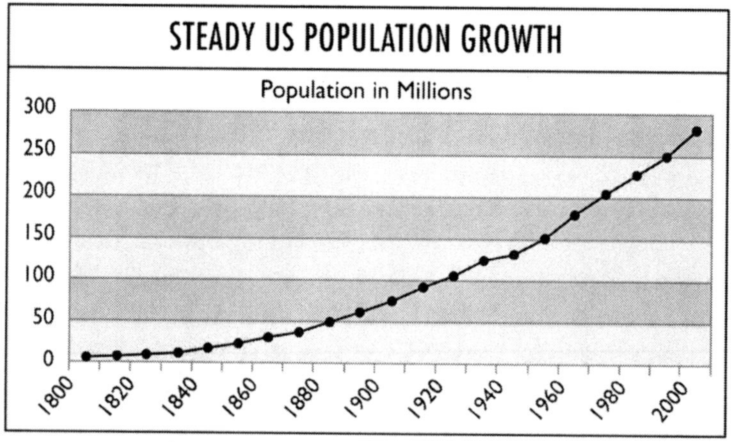

The graphs below track trends in both the national birth rate and in the rate of immigration over the past fifty years. The changes—in short, a steep drop in the birth rate and a steep rise in immigration—tell us all we need to know.

What's truly eye-opening is the drop in the U.S. birth rate. Whether this decline is being caused by economic factors—

raising children is far more time-consuming and expensive in developed countries—or by social factors—primarily the "liberation" of women from the home—in the space of fifty years, our birth rate has been cut in half.

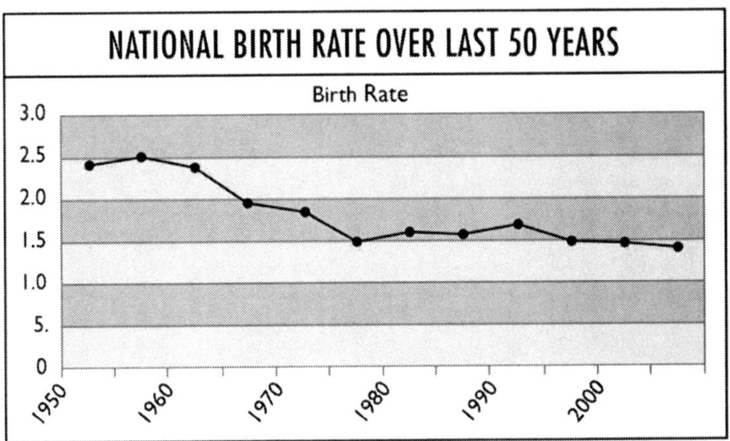

With the birth rate tumbling, it follows that if our population is still growing it must be due to immigration. Since immigration all but came to a halt from the 1930s to the 1950s, or from the Great Depression through the Second World War, it has grown every decade since then, more than doubling from 1950 to 1970, and doubling again from 1970 to 1990. In fact, the number of immigrants in the 1990s—about 12 million—easily eclipsed the previous record of 9 million set in the first decade of the twentieth century.

That all changed after 9/11, and with declining immigration, our population growth has once again fallen into the single digits.

It's also important to recognize that while immigration is responsible for what little population growth we enjoy, the faces of today's immigrants are changing. The immigrants who poured into America at the turn of the nineteenth century were primarily European. Those who arrived at the turn of the twentieth, were mostly Hispanic. In many ways, the earlier

European immigrants landed on an entirely different shore. Back then, the path from Ellis Island to the American middle class was much shorter. Now the manufacturing activity that brought about the personal economic improvement of so many immigrants is in decline.

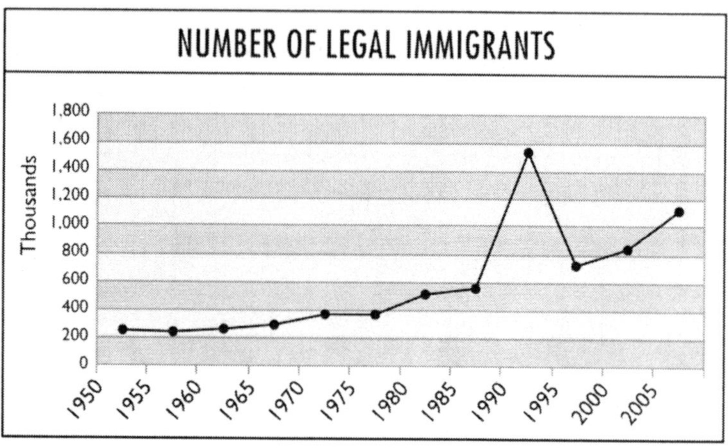

Those manufacturing jobs didn't require a lot of education, and they paid a living wage. Today it's different. Most of the jobs in our economy have grown steadily more complex and technologically demanding. They require more education than many of our kids have gotten. It means that *the bar has been set much higher for those attempting to climb into the middle class today*. If you don't want to spend your life behind a cash register, or under the blistering sun, you need the equivalent of a college education.

That said, the rise in Hispanic immigration does bode well for the labor supply, since the Hispanic birth rate is almost twice that of the general population. Hispanic educational attainment, however, is still much lower than the national average, creating opportunities for forward-thinking communities, which we'll cover later.

In short, while continuing to contribute badly needed workers to the economy, and just as importantly, payroll taxes to the U.S. Treasury, the recent wave of Hispanic immigrants can't be counted on to fill jobs the more highly skilled and better-educated Baby Boomers will leave behind when they retire. And we can't count on importing that talent because most of the countries from which we would get that extra, skilled talent have worse demographics than we do. So the latest surge in immigration won't help us—at least not anytime soon—to avoid the catastrophe of full employment in America's skilled workforce, although it will feed the economy's hunger for labor in the service sector. When we get to Economic Base Theory in Chapter 3, the risks associated with these trends will become even more clear.

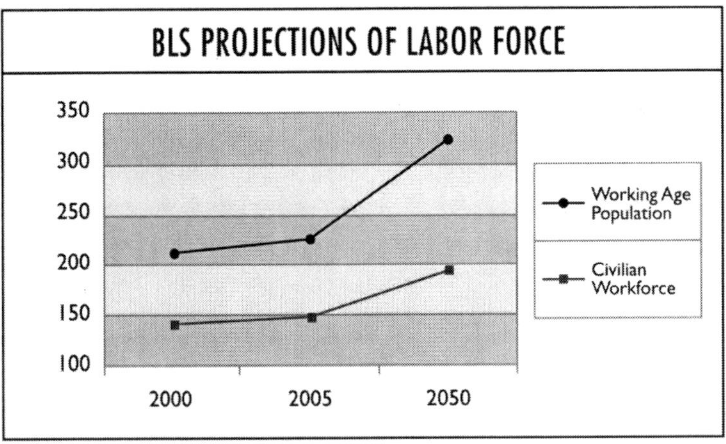

So, between a growing population that will need a growing economy, an abrupt drop in the birth rate, immigration combined with a mass exodus of the most productive workers, let's take a look at how the growth dynamics of the workforce over time affects the Dependency Ratio. The Dependency Ratio is the number of workers in an economy compared to the number of those too old, too young or unable to work.

The graph above shows Bureau of Labor Statistics projections for the American labor force. In 2005, out of a working age population of 226 million, 149 million, or sixty-six percent, were part of the civilian workforce. By the year 2050, the working-age-population will grow to more than 320 million, but only sixty percent, or 195 million, will be part of the civilian workforce.

This will lead to steadily increasing pressure on the shrinking workforce, whose salaries are one of the main sources of federal revenue. As the graph below shows, the economic dependency ratio—or the number of people outside the labor force to every one-hundred people in it—is slowly rising again after having reached zero around the year 2000. And not only will the number of wage earners as a proportion of the total population keep dropping over the next forty years, those outside the workforce will be far older on average than they used to be.

That said, if you look at the left side of the graph, you'll see that the economic dependency ratio was much higher in 1950, when about one-hundred-fifty Americans were outside the workforce for every one-hundred in it. At the time, however, most of those who weren't working were sixteen or younger—only about fifteen percent of them were sixty-five or older.

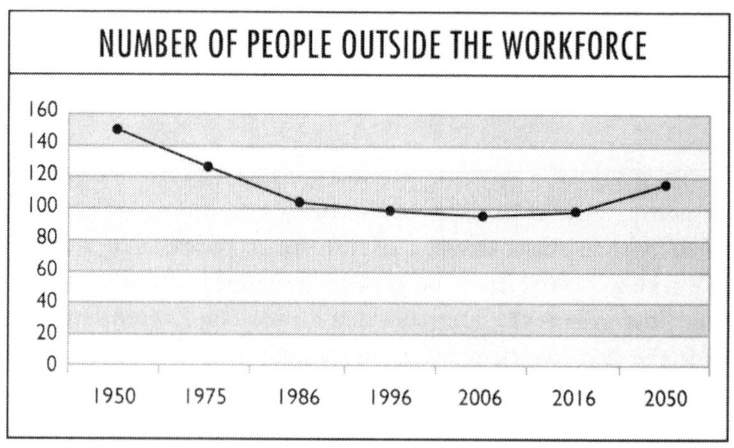

In 2050, according to BLS projections, there will be only one-hundred-fifteen people outside the workforce for every hundred in it, but less than forty-five percent of them will be children—who will go on to find work—and more than thirty-five percent of them will be over the age of sixty-five. While it's true that many Boomers are going to try and work through their sixties and seventies, there is evidence that the sedentary lifestyle and excesses that defined the Me Generation are taking a heavier toll than first thought.

To help illustrate the dynamics of these forces it is useful to visualize your community's population as a pie chart with four sectors; 1. Qualified Workers, 2. Unqualified Workers, 3. Dependents too Old to Work, and 4. Dependents too Young to Work. Over the next twenty-five years, the proportional size of your young and old/dependent sectors and unqualified worker sectors will grow, while your qualified worker sector will shrink.

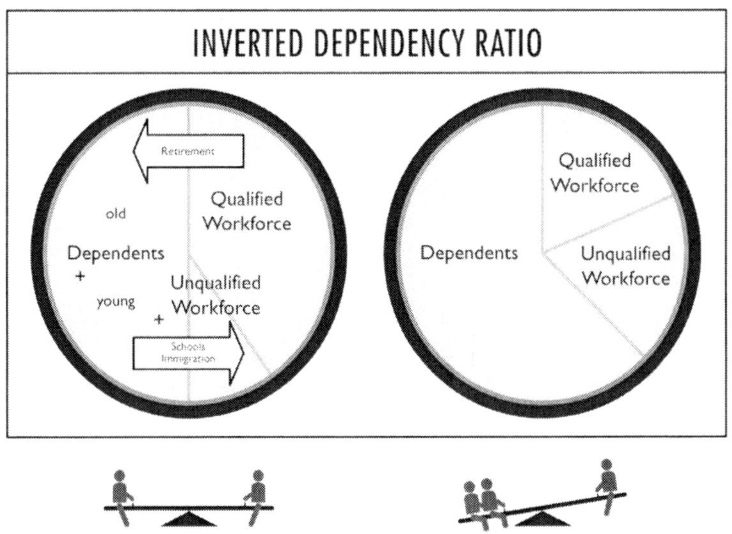

You will have to support more people each year with fewer workers. At some point this will become unsustainable because there won't be enough qualified workers to staff the economy as it wants to grow. Boomers are bailing out of the workforce, leaving the qualified-worker sector and swelling the old/dependents sector.

Too many of an already undersized sector of young dependents are failing to come to the workforce educated and ready to work. They will swell the unqualified sector and starve the economy of the qualified workers needed to grow the economy. All the wrong sectors are growing, and the only sector capable of sustaining the economy is shrinking. In some communities it is shrinking fast.

I'll bet a few pages ago you started thinking of reasons why it probably won't be that bad, or why at least it won't happen to your community. I did the same thing. So let me save you some time. The next chapter lays out the five major mitigating factors that might neutralize or even reverse the effects of the Big Four irreversible forces at the root of our problem. But don't rationalize the problem away until you finish Chapter 3. There we will describe the thirteen aggravating forces making things even worse.

Chapter 2

Mitigating Forces

In 2009, one of my best friends, Art, died suddenly and unexpectedly of a heart attack at age fifty-four. Police found him slumped over the steering wheel of his truck after a morning jog along the Rio Grande. His death was a shock to everyone because he appeared to be so healthy.

Among our circle of friends, he was widely regarded as the most fit. While nowhere near fanatical, he ran, biked and made it to the gym a couple of times a week. He was often my Sunday morning hiking partner, and we went backpacking a couple of times a year together.

He was conscious of his diet, and his easygoing demeanor seemed to make him immune to stress. After the funeral, conversations among our-friends-in-common revealed we were each mulling the same four questions.

How Could this Happen to Someone so Fit?

The autopsy discovered one hundred per cent blockage of one coronary artery, partial blockage of the other, and scar tissue indicating at least two prior heart attacks. He wasn't really healthy or fit. He was a walking time bomb in the advanced stages of heart disease.

Did he know?

I began to recall bits and pieces of our conversations. Two years before when he was still working in Colorado, he had to cancel a backpacking trip we had planned because something was going on in his chest or heart. He didn't have any energy (probably one of the heart attacks). Instead of going on the trip, he went to the emergency room. They did some tests, told him he was fine and sent him home.

On our last hike, his pace was measurably slower and he seemed to be laboring more than usual. I am haunted by a couple of conversations we had on the hiking trail about living a full life. He mentioned that his grandfather and a couple of uncles had died of coronaries in their forties. But his father, at eighty-one, was still bright, active and healthy. A recent checkup showed his blood pressure was a little elevated and his cholesterol was getting to the point where he might have to start taking medication. But on the final office visit after an appendicitis operation two months before he died, the doctor told him he had the heart of a thirty-year-old. While I'm sure that helped him rationalize away his family history and the symptoms, HE KNEW.

Could it Have Been Prevented?

There is a good chance he could have lived another ten or twenty years if he had put his family history and the warning signs together and gone in for more tests. Instead, he knew something was wrong, but the feedback from his appendectomy surgeon and his friends about how healthy he looked gave him the plausible deniability to rationalize and procrastinate. I think it was the fear that an angioplasty would find something that would put him on an operating table where his chest would be cracked open that might have kept him from making the appointment. But even though there was enough data, and he intuitively seemed to know he had a serious problem, he was never able to act on it. In some ways, I think he was the victim of his optimistic outlook on life and his self-image of a strong, fit, healthy, fun-loving guy living life to the max. The fact that it was reinforced every day by people telling him how fit he looked may have kept him from getting the conclusive data he needed to better understand the threat. Which then begs the question:

Am I too at Risk and Don't Know it? Do I Know What I Don't Know?

Or worse, do I know it, but can't somehow come to grips with it in a way that produces corrective action?

The week after the service, my wife booked an appointment with a local cardiologist. In the weeks that followed I found that I was not alone. Many of our friends and acquaintances had signed up too. It struck me later that Art's reaction to the combination of mixed messages and fear is analogous to the reaction people have to the risks of full employment that our communities are facing.

If you are inclined to dismiss full employment as a major problem, this chapter will give you all the reasons you'll need for plausible deniability. But while there are seven factors that could avert or mitigate a long-term labor crisis, there are another thirteen forces that are actually making things worse. In the end, I hope this chapter leaves you worried enough to dig a little deeper, starting with asking if you know what you don't know.

Mitigating Forces

I know you have already started making a list of things that could alleviate, delay or indefinitely postpone the problem, or at least keep it from being catastrophic. There are five major forces that you could use to rationalize demoting full-employment as a problem now or in the future. We have become skilled at rationalizing away big, complicated, scary problems for which we have no obvious or convenient solutions. So I have saved you the trouble. If you need a platform for denial that this is a major game-changing problem worth worrying about, here is the list of excuses in no particular order of importance: **1. Recessions, 2. Immigration, 3. Delayed Retirement, 4. Pandemic, and 5. Increased Productivity**. But keep in mind that there are many more factors making things even worse. These aggravating factors are listed in the table below, and we will go through them in the next chapter.

Causal Forces	Aggravating Forces	Mitigating Forces
*Falling Birth Rate *Boomer Anomaly * Failing Schools *Increased Longevity	* Dropout Rate * Falling Educational Achievement * Rising Educational Threshold * Structural Educational Misalignment * Skill Mismatches * Spiky Forces * Immigration * Boomer Drain * Work Ethic * Polarization * Short-Timers Disease * Capital Destruction	* Recession * Immigration * Delayed Retirement * Pandemic * Increased Productivity

Later, if you attempt to persuade others that they should worry about the likelihood or the consequences of the coming workforce shortage, you are going to want to bring up these five mitigating factors, or excuses, all at once and quickly rebut them with the list of aggravating factors. Otherwise, your audience will be thinking instead of listening. Instead of having a dialogue, you'll run the risk of leaving people feeling litigated and outsmarted instead of convinced and converted. Only if you have a balanced, data-driven sense of your predicament will you care enough to actually do anything about it.

Recession/Depression

I started writing this book in early 2006 before most of us could see the recession coming. My original opening line was, "Barring a prolonged economic recession or depression or a major pandemic, every industrialized nation in the world will run out of the qualified workers needed to staff their economies." It was just my luck that two years into the book we got into the worst economic contraction since the Great Depression. That was followed by predictions of the Swine Flu pandemic.

Who's going to buy the idea that a lack of qualified workers is our biggest problem when the so-called recovery is jobless and 14 million people are still out of work? If it was a little counterintuitive before the recession, now it's more like trying to sell raincoats in the Sub-Sahara.

A prolonged recession mitigates a labor supply in several ways. Besides freeing up 14 million extra workers, this recession has destroyed personal net worth and businesses on a level not seen in seventy-five years. As employers cut back production, they laid off employees, idled equipment and vacated space. Most of this unused capacity will have to be reabsorbed before we start seeing new economic growth.

In many small towns, the most important source of new jobs has been the growth of local governments and tax-dependent institutions. The weak recovery has them delaying hiring, and in many cases, cutting staff even as the demand for services starts to recover. The bottom line is, I don't think we are going to bounce back to full employment as fast this time. But keep in mind that while a recession may push off the day your community reaches full employment, it doesn't push off any birthdays. The aging of the workforce accelerates unabated.

The other thing to remember is that a recession's impact is not uniform or democratic. While the nation's economy struggles to get back to pre-recession production levels, some parts of our country—like Detroit—have been in recession for decades and are now in what could only be described as full-on depression with no end in sight.

Remarkably, there are other communities in the country such as Hobbs, New Mexico, where employment growth, tax revenue and appreciation of home values never got close to going negative. In fact, its economy is still too short of the service workers needed to staff a second or third shift at the local Wal-Mart. Hobbs can look forward to being the first in line to face catastrophic full employment.

Demand Destruction

The recession created another mitigating problem: **demand destruction**. I estimate that in 2005, up to twenty percent of the U.S. economy was fake. It was built on consumption financed by debt by borrowers who had no way to pay it back. This part of our economy was never real. So don't expect to see it bounce back in the recovery. Translation: a lot of jobs won't come back.

Given that the fact that our credit system still isn't fixed, our community banks are disappearing, and the world's central banks are printing money like crazy, I figure we are looking at something between the prolonged stagnation similar to what the Japanese have endured and—in the worst case scenario—the collapse of Western Civilization.

When my wife and I sat down and looked at what we really needed to survive and live a decent life, we realized that over half of what we have, and much of what we consume, we really don't need. It was a revelation. We cut way back. So have others. Everyone is learning to do more with less. So beyond the destruction of the fake economy, we are likely to see an additional chunk of the future economy permanently destroyed by a Thrift Shift phenomena, which will further delay a return to previous production (employment) levels and further delay full employment.

Another factor contributing to the Thrift Shift is that, with the exception of health care, old people don't buy as much stuff. As 78 million Boomer-geezers become an increasing share of the population, consumption—demand and employment—could be depressed, maybe substantially.

Another factor may turn out to be a less materialistic and more conservative incoming generation. I see signs that my twenty-and-thirty-something children may have been traumatized enough by the Great Recession in the same way my grandparents were by the Great Depression.

The long and deep nature of the recession means it will take longer to get to full employment. It's not something to wish for, but it is a potential consolation for those of us who are already concerned about catastrophic full employment.

Another casualty of the recession was retirement plans. Some 401(k)s have lost as much as fifty percent of their value, causing many retirements to be rescheduled or cancelled.

Delayed Retirement

Hey, the Boomers created this problem by not having enough kids and letting the public school system rot, so don't let them retire, and let's make them work until they drop. If we ever get back to full employment, all we have to do is raise the retirement age to eighty-five, right?

Retirement expectations of the Boomers are in stark contrast to those of our parents. Few Boomers expect to get a gold watch at sixty-five, take a trip around the world, buy a condo on a golf course and sit around waiting for the grandchildren to visit. Many Boomers have already retired in their fifties. Many Boomers are going to find it impossible to turn their brains off at sixty-five or seventy. Because today's careers are more brainwork, and Boomers are healthier than their ancestors, many will be able to stay on the job. Some who find their work too satisfying and purposeful to retire will power on to the grave. Others plan to slow down, gradually retire in some capacity, or return to service as a consultant for a while. Others may be called to second careers as teachers and health care workers.

In the end, Boomers who tell you they plan to work to the grave, and those professing to retire as soon as they are eligible are probably both kidding themselves. Be wary of opinion surveys of retirement expectations. They more often represent wishful thinking rather than realistic planning. Many of the jobs Boomers say they are going to stay working at won't even exist in ten years. Many more won't have the physical stamina after age sixty to keep working.

Like all species, human beings have a life span determined by our DNA. Unfortunately in this case, as we approach our fifties, around the time we should be done raising our kids, a genetic trigger flips slowly shutting down production of testosterone, estrogen and HGH, and slowing the body's ability to rejuvenate. Good genes, diet and exercise can go a long way to keeping one strong and sharp in their later years, but every year it gets harder to stay physically strong and mentally sharp. You can't keep muscle mass even lifting weights three times a week. Your eyesight goes, your hearing degrades, you lose half your taste buds, your brain steadily shrinks, and you get grumpy and complain about the government all the time.

It's Mother Nature's way of saying she is done with us. The primary mission of the species is to reproduce. After age fifty, the species doesn't need us anymore. In the past, we became a liability after we raised our kids. In the years ahead, though, nothing could be further from the truth. Most of our economies aren't going to be able to grow if the elders check out too soon. But you should curb your expectations for forcing geezers to work longer. Many won't be able to. In many cases it could be more trouble than it'll be worth. Advances in brain science promise some startling advances in maintaining and even elevating brain function in older people. I hope they hurry.

Immigration

If we can't force enough geezers to stay on to fill the gaps, all we have to do is open up Ellis Island again and give a green card or citizenship to anyone with the experience, education and language skills we need, right? After all, that's what we did in the past when we had a frontier to settle and railroads and cities to build. Immigration is a tough subject these days, but it always has been. On one hand, I've always thought, "There are honest, hard-working Mexican nationals willing to walk seven hunderd miles through the Chihuahuan desert to work here for $6 an hour, and we're trying to stop them?"

But the notion that all we have to do is open up the borders to solve our long-term labor deficit is naive for several reasons. First, we are not necessarily going to be short of unskilled workers; we are going to be short of *qualified* workers. Unless something changes, we are going to continue to see relatively high unemployment rates among the unskilled and uneducated. At the end of 2010, the jobless rate for those without a high school diploma was more than three times higher than for those with a college degree. Immigration of uneducated, unskilled and unprepared-to-learn people will only make things worse. At the present time, national security concerns and the recession have reduced legal and illegal immigration.

The other problem with the immigration solution is the fact that most of the countries from which we might get the extra, qualified workers are in much worse demographic shape than we are.

Were it not for the recent repatriation of the Eastern Bloc workforce and immigration from Africa and the Middle East, Europe's economy would have hit catastrophic full employment years ago.

Russia appears to be in the worst situation. Its birth rate is a dismal 1.4 children per fertile female, and still dropping. Russia also has the distinction of being the only industrialized country whose life expectancy is also dropping. Sometimes referred to as a Malthusian Hell, Russia's population has been shrinking by 750,000 every year. The problem is so bad that the Russian government has resorted to public campaigns to spur procreation. They have a national procreation holiday where people of child-bearing age are given the day off to screw around, literally.

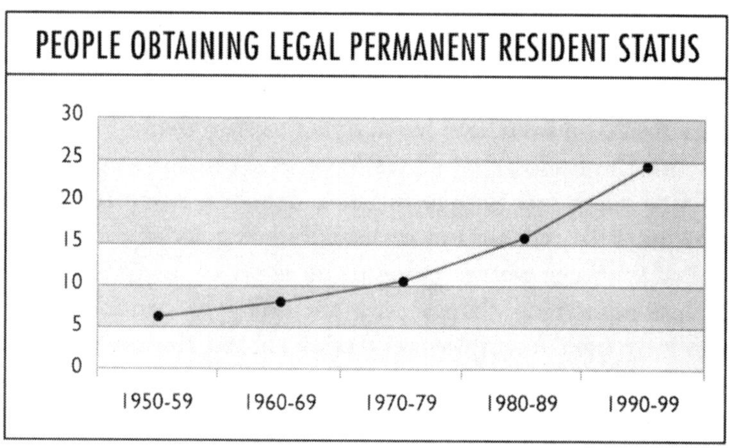

Over the last forty years, China restricted couples to one child and aborted up to twenty percent of its girls. So today they don't have enough women to have enough babies to catch up. Expect them to run out of workers and for their economy begin to flat-line around 2015. Think they are going to let us have any of their talent? They have what is now called a 4:2:1 dilemma. Instead of four children being born each generation to support two parents and one grandparent, the reverse is happening. One child, probably a spoiled boy, is going to have to support and care for his two parents and four grandparents.

The Japanese are in big trouble too. Their birth rate has been among the lowest in the industrialized world at 1.4. That has prompted the national government to give every family the equivalent of $80,000 on the birth of their fourth child. They have an even bigger problem on the other end with the highest life expectancy at eighty-eight, and improving. Their population is becoming so unbalanced with elders and imminent retirees that Japanese developers have been out looking for sites in foreign countries where they can offshore their elderly.

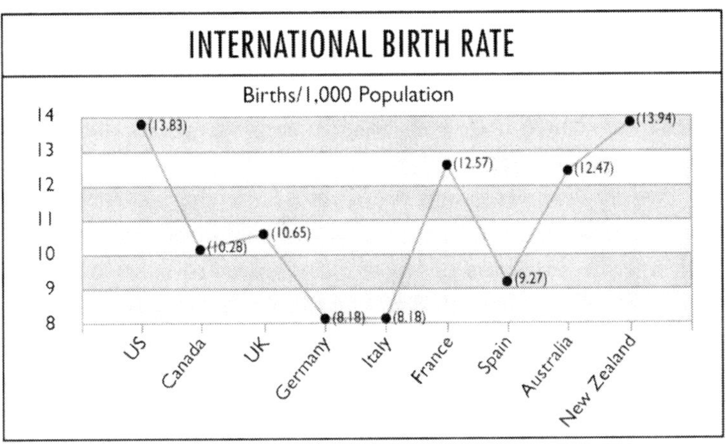

One such developer I talked with in 2005 actually used the term "Extended Stay Community" to describe the project. Their development plan proposed an active adult community, an assisted-living facility, nursing homes and hospice in a linear pattern across the site. After they left, one of my staff jokingly asked if we might get them to buy more land if we added sites for a funeral home and graveyard. The point is, they don't have room on their already crowded island, and they are going to have to put all their old people somewhere.

Third-world countries are even less able to afford losing their educated and skilled workers. Given the dire straits the world labor market will be in by 2020, I wouldn't be surprised to see talent flows to and from nations become a major flashpoint for international conflict.

With most of the industrialized world in worse shape than we are, it may be wishful thinking that we can steal enough qualified workers to make up our deficit. Instead, we should start worrying about the rest of the world stealing ours.

Increased Productivity

Technology will save us. The pace of technological innovation and the evolution of newer, more efficient business models should permit each worker to produce more goods and services so we won't need as many workers, the logic goes. Having a lower percentage of qualified workers won't be a problem because they will be able to produce so much more in the future than they can now.

Twenty-five years ago we didn't have the microchip, personal computers, the internet or cellular communications. It took a while for some of these innovations to actually increase our productivity. But no one can deny that they have made us profoundly more productive. If the pace of technological innovation is actually accelerating like everyone says, then we have nothing to worry about, right? Promising advances in brain science, bio-technology and material science alone could close the gap.

U.S. workers are the most productive in the world, with output per worker topping $63,800 per year.

Because of the inertia of the workplace and the pace of business and product cycles, it has been difficult to sustain productivity gains of more than two percent annually over time. We are going to need quantum leaps in productivity if we are going to run a bigger economy with fewer and fewer qualified workers.

New business models will also help. The accompanying effects of creative destruction will free up talent along the way and improve the labor supply situation.

Mass customization, distributed work strategies, virtual project team models are already a reality.

In addition to the steady release of talent from the effects of creative destruction—where innovation makes goods, services and processes obsolete—there is tremendous potential for regulatory reform to free up large numbers of highly educated workers. Think how many bookkeepers, CPAs, tax attorneys and IRS agents would be freed up if we just simplified the tax code. Shifting all that defensive work to offense would not only jack up the productivity of every enterprise, it would free up millions of talented, well-educated, and hard-working residents in every town.

The promise of productivity increases, accelerating technological innovation and new business models, combined with the potential for regulatory reforms to free up new pools of talent should give us all comfort.

Pandemic

And then there is always Mother Nature's ultimate solution: a pandemic that wipes out everyone over seventy. They say a major pandemic is imminent—in fact, overdue. You could also put the threat of a biological attack or an act of terrorism in this category. And when it happens, it could wipe out enough of the elderly population to re-balance the population. Problem solved.

Except that we would likely lose a proportional number of children as well—our future workers. One might come away from this thinking that there are enough mitigating factors in play to quell any practical concern that full employment is something we should spend time worrying about. Before you do, there is another, longer list of factors that promise to make things even worse.

Chapter 3

Aggravating Forces

The Dropout Rate

The most important aggravating factor, and certainly the most shameful, is our high school dropout rate. If we don't find a way to get the thirty to fifty percent of our high school students that dropout to stay in school, there is no way for the U.S. to remain the world's leading economy. In fact, before it's over, I predict it will become a major national security issue. When people begin to realize that the biggest threat to our country, our communities and way of life is our inability to staff the economy, things will start to change. Until then, it looks like a daunting task—getting kids who don't like school and don't see the value in it to not only keep going, *but to take the harder subjects they need to be employable.*

Falling Educational Achievement

National statistics show that educational *attainment* has been on the rise recently in some school districts. But that's meaningless if educational *achievement* continues to fall. If we pass kids to help their self-esteem, or to make the school district's numbers look better for future funding, this dumbing down of the system will take—is taking—our workforce the wrong way. It's diluting the value of education at a time when the value of an education should be going up.

Educational *achievement* is the measure of what a student or potential worker has learned—skill or knowledge—versus what diploma or what piece of paper a school might have granted them to get them out of the system. The result of dumbing down curriculum and lowering standards has the same negative effect on the future economy as driving up the dropout rate. Failing to raise curriculum standards fast enough to match the needs of employers is one of the fine-print issues lost in the discussion.

The Rising Education Threshold for Work Readiness

What makes the dropout rate and falling achievement levels especially damaging is that the skill and education threshold for work is rising every year as work becomes more complex and technologically sophisticated. We're demanding that workers know more and have better analytical thinking and communication skills to be able to work better, faster and smarter every year. As employers struggle to boost productivity to stay competitive, the bar for employees is being raised higher. In the end, there are only two ways for a business or a worker to become more productive: invest in new equipment and technology, or invest in additional education and training.

Productivity gains by U.S. employers over the last twenty years have outpaced other industrialized countries because we outspent them on new equipment and training. As a result, the education, skill and knowledge required for work in our economy is the highest in the world and is going up every year. When I graduated from high school in 1967, even if you were in the dumb math class and barely passing English, you could walk across the street the day after graduation and go to work in an auto repair garage as a mechanic's helper, and in three years you could be earning enough to support a family of four. Today, you practically need an electrical engineering degree just to open the hood of a car. Many so-called blue-collar technician positions now require workers whose brains are wired to do math at the Algebra II or pre-calculus level. If they're not, those workers won't be able to intellectualize the troubleshooting protocols to repair the copier in your office.

If the educational standards for work continue to advance faster than the educational achievement of our new workers, we will fall further behind every year, making the shortages of qualified workers even more severe.

Structural Misalignment between our Education System and the Needs of the Future Economy

While some progress has been made in organizing career paths and school-to-work programs, much more needs to be done in those areas. We have to try to predict what industries and jobs will be short of qualified workers in the future so we can strategically move resources to customize curriculum, build program capacity and steer students and mid-career-change candidates to those fields.

But that type of planning is considered heresy by the leadership and the rank-and-file of the education profession. In the past, it really didn't matter if half the graduating class went off to become anthropologists. If you wanted to be an anthropologist, God bless you, because we had an oversupply of engineers, nurses, and lawyers. It didn't hurt anyone.

For the average person, the next door neighbor's, or the Black or Hispanic population's inability to educate more of their children was a humanitarian problem. You had to get into the abstract economics of the general costs to society of steadily increasing prison populations and such if you wanted to make an economic case that an uneducated segment of society was a major threat to anyone but themselves.

If the family across the street failed to get their kids to school ready to learn, and allowed them to drop out, it was regrettable, and you might have felt badly for them, but it was not a direct economic threat to you and yours. In fact, it just meant less competition for you.

This new era is changing all that. We will need our educational institutions to have a much better sense of the future job market for their service area and for their local and regional economies than they have ever had because we cannot afford to waste scarce public and private resources to educate one hundred times more anthropologists than we need.

A bigger problem, however, is the philosophical position held by a majority of the education profession. They are hell-bent to resist any attempt by the business community to tailor general education programs and curriculum to more directly meet the needs of the private sector, especially a particular industry.

The Mismatch of Skills and Experience to Jobs of the Future

Another major problem is the mismatch of education and skill levels of the workforce and the jobs in demand. In the past, this has always been a problem, especially for regions of the country or communities where whole industries declined or evaporated, leaving large pools of skilled people unemployed and on their own to migrate or find new careers. These unemployed workers were a common target for economic developers and workforce developers. These pools of qualified workers either moved to other markets where their skills were in demand, or they gravitated toward other local employers that needed their transferable skills. As the global economy becomes more volatile, these pools of workers will become more common.

The Spiky Forces

Talent—meaning qualified workers—is not evenly distributed. Some communities produce their own talent and act as talent magnets, attracting even more talent from other places. On the other end of the scale there are places that have a difficult time keeping their kids in school and don't have the institutional resources needed for working-age people to get the training and education they need to move up or to change careers. These communities experience a continual brain drain—where anytime anyone gets a chance they leave. The Spiky Force is a phenomenon chronicled in Richard Florida's book *Who's your City*. He describes recent demographic migration patterns of the most productive and creative people in the world, and developed a map that graphically demonstrates where talented, highly-educated people are concentrating, and where they are not.

The bottom line is that talent is migrating from certain types of communities and congregating in others. The brightest gravitate to areas where the amenities for their lifestyle, and the most productive business and social ecosystems are being developed to support them. This migration of talent will make it increasingly difficult to rationalize investment in a superior education system when your graduates move to competing communities in droves.

Housing Impeded Mobility of Workers

Many of our dislocated workers who've been turned loose by an industry or company try to move to other communities, but they find it difficult to sell their homes or get enough money to finance their relocation. This is especially true right now.

It's particularly dangerous in this new era when a community turns a large pool of talent into footloose workers. If the community cannot find new jobs for those people, it will lose a critical mass of workers needed to sustain itself.

The same kind of damage will be done to the community by its educational and workforce training institutions if they don't become strategic.

Immigration - Why Opening up Ellis Island Again Won't Work This Time

Most developed, and many of developing countries we would expect to provide us the extra qualified workers to fill the gaps left by retiring Boomers are facing demographic conditions worse than we are. Europe, Japan, Canada, Australia, Russia and even China have seen their birth rates fall lower than ours.

Qualified labor could eventually replace oil as the primary strategic resource for modern economies. The issue of immigrating talent from one economy or trading bloc to another could ignite the next major war. We might see a time soon when foreign employers start outbidding U.S. firms for our own talent.

The Boomer Brain Drain

Another factor making the situation worse is the Boomer Brain Drain. Boomers are the hardest working, best educated, most productive class of workers in the economy, and when they go they will take with them tribal knowledge and experience that can't be replaced. The loss of the most experienced and productive from the ranks of our educational institutions and businesses will leave management gaps, disrupt production and wreak havoc on companies that have not planned well. For example, in 2008, the U.S. Department of Energy had 188,000 full-time employees among their forty-one agencies. An incredible seventy percent of its total workforce was eligible to retire that year, and it had an eight percent retention rate for new hires after three years. You might say that the DOE is the poster child for our dilemma.

When you consider that the DOE is responsible for solving global warming, fixing the power grid and getting us off foreign oil so we stop funding the guys we're fighting, the agency looks to be at great risk. It looks like there is no way it can sustain itself. How will it manage these programs without making major changes in the way it operates?

Work Ethic

One reason for the DOE's low new-hire-retention rate is the combination of an entrenched bureaucratic and ritualistic workplace culture combined with starkly different attitudes and values about work-and-life-balance by the generations that have followed the Boomers.

The attitudes of the newer generations of workers have been well documented. I'm sure our parents were thinking the same things about us in the 1960s. We ended up working harder and longer than our parents. So maybe it's only temporary. Maybe we're judging too soon. What's really different about these new generations of workers is that the Boomers were converted from flower children to workaholics when they realized that working harder and longer was the only way to find and keep a good job. It will be the reverse for our children.

Incoming generations are going to have to pick up some serious slack if they want to live in an improving economy.

The Clash of Competing Worldviews,

One of the most troubling forces affecting our ability to deal with this problem is the profound disconnect between the business and education worlds. Over the last several decades, the disconnect has developed from a "you do your job and let us do ours" attitude, to one of open mutual disrespect and all-out hostility, with each side blaming the other for their inability to do their jobs. Now it's like one of those bitter marriages that went bad years ago, but divorce is not an option, so they continue to live together under the pretense of shared responsibility, motivated increasingly by anger, resentment and the occasional opportunity to punish the other. In most places these two groups are so philosophically and politically polarized they can no longer communicate. In fact, when they are forced to, they just antagonize each other.

People who have chosen commerce vocations either start out with, or develop a worldview substantially at odds with their neighbors who chose vocations focused directly on improving the health, education or welfare of human beings.

The worldview of the archetypical business person goes something like this: "I've invested everything I have in my business, mortgaged every asset for working capital, and put my family's future at risk every day in an increasingly volatile, cutthroat global economy to make a measly four percent profit margin. Every year my suppliers raise their prices, my competitors lower theirs, and the government raises my taxes and buries me in more regulations."

Business owners live in a constant state of entrepreneurial anxiety that at any moment they will have to close or downsize and lay off the people who've made their business work and who've depended on them to feed and care for their families. They see public employees, especially unionized teachers and tenured higher education faculty and their administrators, as a protected class of bureaucrats who neither understand nor care how the economy works.

They think most teachers defaulted into education degrees in college after washing out of more rigorous programs like business and engineering. They are convinced that teachers and social workers believe that business owners are driven by greed and are the cause of most of society's problems. Business people hold the education profession personally responsible for the decline of the nation's public schools and the fact that they can't find anyone to fill open positions that can read, calculate or pass a drug test.

On the other side, educators, like their allies in the health and social services professions, have chosen to dedicate their lives to helping and nurturing people directly, especially those least able to help themselves and in greatest need. They knowingly sacrificed higher salaries for more meaningful and satisfying work and job security.

Teachers in particular believe that they are part of a highly-evolved, scientifically-based profession that elevates them from others without formal pedagogical training. They feel betrayed, unrewarded and unappreciated by society, and rail at the thought of a colleague with a master's degree in education making less than many blue-collar technicians with a year or two of trade school.

Educators believe the public education system is in trouble because business people don't appreciate the value of a well-educated workforce. They think that the exploitative way employers use people makes it harder to motivate students and convince voters and legislators to invest in education. They see the business lobby using their virtually unlimited financial resources to buy political influence to use against them, blocking every worthy reform and funding proposal to keep from paying their fair share.

In short, the reason our public education system, and most of our other social indicators have not improved is the fault of greed-driven business interests and a political system corrupted by their money and power.

These diametrically opposed worldviews will need to be reconciled before any of the major changes needed in our school system can be implemented. Until the teachers learn more about how the economy works, and understand the plight of the investor-entrepreneur, and until the business owners and managers better understand how difficult and expensive it is to educate kids, progress will be too slow and episodic to move the needle on our long-term Inverted Labor Supply problem.

At the moment, they don't use the same nomenclature, they don't have a common standard for work readiness, and they don't have common methodologies and data they both can trust. In most places, they don't go to each other's conferences, and they have no representation on each other's governing boards. They are not just having trouble communicating; they aren't talking to each other.

Short-Timers Disease

Another big problem is what I call Short-Timers Disease. The overwhelming majority of people in positions of influence or power are Boomers who are within a few years of retirement.

After spending their careers fighting their way to the top of the food chain, the last thing they want to do is pull a ninety-degree-bank turn a few years from retirement, especially when the trouble isn't going to hit hard until after their watch. These are people who control the budgets and the institutions that have to do these heavy lifts.

As a broad categorical group, they are the least likely to consider change. They're not going to do it, they don't know how, and don't want to rock the boat. Short-Timers don't want to change anything. They are there to just ride it out.

My experience in talking to business and workforce development groups is that they are usually a sea of grey hair, and they don't have the time, knowledge, energy or the will to do anything about these upcoming problems.

Change will be slow, but when it finally comes there will be hell to pay. Organization managers are going to find themselves under a great deal more pressure to make the big institutional changes needed to solve these problems.

When minority students and workers realize that the reasons they're not getting good jobs is no longer prejudice in the workforce, but the failure of their schools to educate them, there will be hell to pay.

When the business community and the institutions that rely on the tax revenue they produce realize that their survival is threatened by the failure of the educational, workforce development and social services institutions, there will be hell to pay. There will be a demand for change.

Flattening Forces

The flattening forces make the economy more volatile, increase the speed of creative destruction, and make it more difficult for employers, students and mid-career change candidates to form long-term career expectations. Recent statistics show that eighty percent of the jobs you will have in the future don't even exist yet.

So how do you expect a community, workforce development group, student or a mid-career change candidate to make a long-term investment for a specific career? This makes it harder to motivate and guide workers about where to invest, and indecision is usually followed by inaction.

Capital Destruction

The recession has two edges. To our advantage, the recession has given us a few more years or months before we hit the death spiral. It has also purged the economy of many inefficient and wasteful jobs in the private sector, and is forcing millions of people in the U.S. to rethink how they live and what they need. This recalibration may depress demand enough to keep some communities from going to the brink of their workforce capacity.

On the other hand, the Great Recession has done two other things: It has demoralized millions of people and prevented them from making the kind of investments in education and training that come from an optimistic economic outlook. It has also wiped out trillions of dollars of net worth.

That is leading to contraction of local tax bases, and ultimately the discretionary tax revenue required to make some of these heavy lifts. If housing prices fall and remain low, if natural gas prices fall with consumption and people buy less, tax revenues will suffer proportionately, making it harder for communities to find the discretionary income to improve, creating a much fiercer environment for sorting out public financing priorities.

Beware the Rise of the Goat Killers

During my Peace Corps assignment in Chile in 1973, our in-country director, Eliseo Carrasco, was trying to give our incoming class of volunteers some insight into the mentality of poverty and the problems it creates, especially in a country being torn apart by class struggle.

He told us this story. A feudal king, alarmed by reports of increasing civil discord among his subjects, decided to ride out into the countryside to see for himself. He came to a peasant tilling his field. To get the peasant to level with him about what was really going on in the realm, the king promised to grant him one wish.

Panicked and unable to think, the farmer looked over at his neighbor's farm a hundred yards away and said, "Okay, my neighbor has ten goats and I only have three." Not hearing a specific wish, the king prodded, "So you would like twenty goats so you would have twice as many as he does, something like that?" The farmer shot back, "No, I want you to kill seven of his."

The king was shocked and deeply saddened that his people were so demoralized and prone to self-destruction. With so many "Goat Killers" out there he knew that things were about to get ugly. Since he couldn't think of anything he could do about it, he began preparing for an insurrection.

We Americans probably still carry the Goat Killing gene, but it has been suppressed by two hundred years of continuous economic expansion.

Go back to the original premise of the Temple of Doom room. You have a falling birth rate, the Boomer Bubble and rising life expectancy putting a twenty-five-year squeeze on the economic viability of our economies and communities. This

Temple of Doom room is closing in on at least half of us. You will be tempted to dismiss the problem. Don't.

Depending on where you are, the mix and relative impact of these factors are going to vary. If you are responsible for your community's economic health, or that of a local tax-dependent institution, you don't want to dismiss this problem without getting more data. If you're honest with yourself and your constituents, you will ask the question, "Do I know what I don't know?"

My friend Art cared about communities and understood the importance of managing their economies. He would feel good about my telling his story if it helped get some of you in for an overdue physical and helped you get your community in for an demographic checkup.

So do it.

Part Two

How Communities Really Work

OPERATIONAL DEFINITION OF ECONOMIC DEVELOPMENT

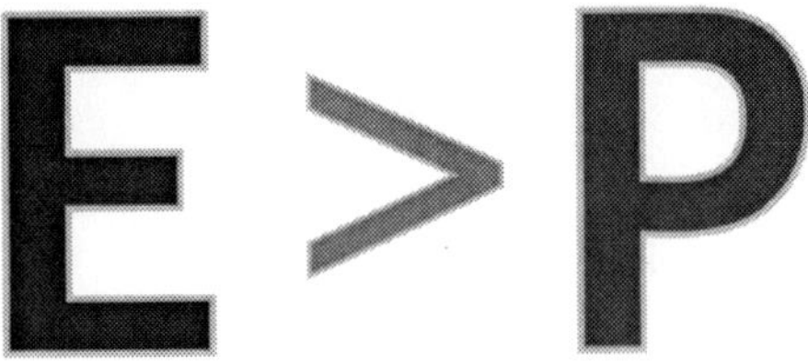

E = Economy | P = Population

Chapter 4

Why Communities are Important

The goal of this chapter is to convince you that the community you live in will have more to do with how well your life goes the next twenty-five years than any other factor you have control over.

Defining Community

Before we launch into a discussion about communities, we need to stop and consider how you are defining it. It doesn't mean the same thing to everyone. In fact, you may change your definition depending on the context or the audience. Community is a pretty loosely defined term, and we will need to tighten up the definition when we start talking about data. Later, when you start trying to gather data, being able to define the community precisely will become important, but right now we are talking about community in the general sense. For now it is whatever you want it to be beyond a neighborhood, and short of a region or megalopolis.

For the sake of discussion, your "community" should have an obvious geographical boundary, and you should be able to tell when you have arrived and when you have left. It should be big and diverse enough to have its own economic or submarket dynamics. And it should have leaders and conform to at least one political jurisdiction collecting tax revenue for public services.

Platforms for Life and Civilization

Communities are the primary platform for the civilization of the human species. It's difficult to overstate the importance of communities to the development of human beings. They are where we are born, grow up, make friends, build our careers, find our mates and raise our families. They are the source of the adage, "It takes a village." Communities are where our lives happen, where we learn how to be human. Our past, present and our potential are profoundly dependent on this real estate platform, this organization of people, this thing we call our community.

Personal Identity

Where you live, where you were born and where you have lived during your life are central to who you are. When we meet someone for the first time we usually ask where they're from before we ask their name, occupation or family details. How you answer the question "Where are you from?" not only defines you, but it may have a lot to do with who you become.

Deep down we know that communities are important to us. Think about how you feel when an outsider goes off on how our community sucks. It's hard not to take it personally. After all, they are implying that all of us suck.

It's even worse when someone in the community goes negative. Given the steady drumbeat of "Ain't it awful" reporting by our local newspapers, TV stations and bloggers, it's a wonder that we can muster any affection for our hometowns.

Most of us take our communities for granted until we have to vote for a bond issue, or the neighborhood starts to organize to fight a new Wal-Mart. Most of us don't have a reason to think analytically about the community we live in and the role it plays in our lives until something bad happens, like your house gets broken into for the third time or you lose your job and have to think about moving.

Friends, Mates and Family

Communities are where we still make most of our friends, find mates, and raise our families. The proximity of supportive family members, circle of friends, the quality of the nightlife, and good public schools will weigh heavily on a person's sense of satisfaction with their community depending on where they are in life.

Career & Education

Whether you work out of a home office, factory, office, store, or at a Starbucks, or you are looking for a job, your community plays a crucial platform role. How much time you spend in traffic, how fast your internet access is, the level of access to business services and your access to continuing education are determined by your community.

Health

Your access to health care, how much exercise you get, and to a certain extent, your diet, are all influenced by where you live. The extent to which you feel connected to your culture is largely dependent on your community.

Net worth

The community we live in will have a major impact on how much we earn, our cost of living, how much we are taxed, and ultimately, our net worth.

Safety

Your security is at stake depending on where you live, too. Property and personal crime varies widely from community to community, as do the chances of getting wiped out by a hurricane, tornado, wildfire, flood or earthquake.

Lifestyle

Lifestyle is a big determinant too. How connected you feel to a place, and how accepted you and others like you feel is a major factor.

There are those who think that the virtual communities we are creating make the places we live in less important. In many ways, that's true. Many of the things we depended on our communities to provide in the past we now can get with a click of the mouse.

In Richard Florida's blockbuster book, *The Rise of the Creative Class,* he refuted a growing notion that the "work from anywhere anytime" age of the internet was making where you live irrelevant. Instead, he asserted that it makes place even more important. If he is right, and I think he is, people are going to need to take the quality, character and future of their communities more seriously than they have in the past. In that book, Florida documented a new class of knowledge workers that is larger and growing faster than anyone suspected.

His thesis proposed that this new class of workers is now the most important and most mobile cohort for the economy, and that they have very different attitudes, values and work habits than their predecessors. Equally important, they are on the move, leaving communities with certain characteristics, and migrating to destination communities with characteristics they need and want.

The message to employers is if you need these creative workers to build your business, you better figure out what makes them tick and then adapt your company work rules, or prepare to lose them to your competition. The message to community leaders and economic developers is if the companies that you expect to build your community's future economy around will require these creative workers, you better figure out which community characteristics are driving them off, and which are attracting them.

It's not just Richard Florida's "creative class" workers that are on the move, though. One of the game-changing facts of a zero-sum labor market is that the workers in short demand have the power. They will eventually be able to work anywhere they want. Take a minute and think about that—ANYWHERE THEY WANT!

This was a pretty disruptive idea, especially for the economic developers working for communities with repellent profiles. The ones with winning profiles rejoiced, and they continue to recruit. The economic development profession never recovered, though. Few could figure out how to morph their traditional corporate recruiting programs into creative-worker-attraction programs, and they still haven't.

Half the economic development conferences around the country since 2000 have been titled "Marketing to the Innovation Economy," or something like it. You can tell by the presentations that no one knows what the Innovation Economy even is, or if they do know, they haven't a clue about how to market to it.

Florida's latest book, *Who's Your City?,* raises the stakes for communities even higher by arguing that when it comes to overall happiness, where you choose to live may be the most important decision you make in life, more important than who you marry, or the career field you choose. "Sorry, Honey, but the man says where we live is more important to my happiness than you are." Oh boy!

Happiness

Happiness is a lot harder to measure objectively than net

worth, but happiness researchers have developed five general factors to measure how the place we live in affects our happiness. Apparently, every complaint or aspiration you can come up with about where you live fits into one of these five categories: 1. Physical and economic security, 2. Basic services, 3. Leadership, 4. Openness, and 5. Aesthetics.

Of course, everyone has slightly different criteria for happiness, and it changes throughout our lives. But you won't be surprised that behavioral psychologists have identified five distinct personality types that may help us sort out what kinds of places make which people happy or sad. Being able to predict which places will make which people happy could be pretty useful, except, of course, for those who like being miserable.

I grew up in Seattle where we would go months without seeing the sun. After spending part of a winter working on the Alaskan Pipeline a hundred miles north of the Arctic Circle, I knew I needed to live somewhere sunny in order to be happy. Starting in November, brawls in the cafeterias and the game rooms increased in frequency. The cause of this phenomenon is now referred to as Seasonal Adjustment Disorder (SAD).

I went to college in New Mexico, where we have almost the same number of sunny days as Seattle has overcast ones. I've never understood why people with SAD live in the dark, gloomy climates when they can live in places like Albuquerque. As a corollary, I can't understand why anyone with a choice stays in a place that isn't good for them, especially places that are in obvious decline, corrupt, dangerous, expensive, polluted and no fun.

CFE - Bush League Factor

There is a factor that multiplies Richard Florida's arguments that the quality and character of places are going to matter even more. In the zero-sum labor environment ahead, communities that can't grow, attract and hold the talent they need to keep their economies in balance with their populations, will be unable to sustain you at the level to which you have become accustomed.

It will be like a sports league with no organizational rules. If there are twenty teams and no provisions or authority to keep the talent evenly spread, then all the good players are going to want to be on the best teams.

No one will want to play for the losing teams, and the games will get more lopsided. Not only will it not be fair, but teams will eventually quit or resort to cheating. Either way, our communities are going to be unwitting participants in an economic bush league.

If this is the league we are going to be playing in, then what team (community) you are on is going to be even more important to your career than ever before. It behooves everyone to try and figure out where their community is going to be in the standings, because if you end up in the cellar, you may never get out. And you don't want everything you have in the world invested in a losing team that's destined to get weaker every year.

Who Comes? Who Goes?

With this crucial creative class of workers needed to staff community economies on the move and leaving unattractive communities for attractive ones, whether you live in an attractive one is increasing in importance.

When you factor in Florida's argument that your choice of community is the most important choice you make in life, the stakes are raised even more.

The Inverted Labor Supply Curve raises the stakes and changes the fundamentals of the game. Before, the risks were marginal. You might not end up in a place as good as you wanted, and you could always move. In this new labor-constrained league, with no commissioner to balance the teams, the wrong choice will be disastrous. This new league doesn't just leave the have-nots behind; it turns them into Goat Killers.

So you are going to want to know, even predict, who is here now, who comes, who goes, who stays and why.

e-community.com

Companies pay site-selection consultants millions of dollars every year to investigate and evaluate communities for future locations. Why don't individuals do the same? While every magazine dealing with finances or lifestyles feels compelled to run a "top ten best places to live" feature of some kind every year, they rarely tell you the criteria they used or how they were developed.

There are a few websites attempting to match personal profiles with compatible community profiles. Eventually they may be as good as E-Harmony.com, Monster.com, and some of the other compatibility sites.

If where you live is more important than who you marry, what career you choose or your net worth, then why is there so little information about communities? Okay. Most of us don't run FBI background checks or compatibility screens on our fiancés, even though it would save some people a lot of time, money and heartache.

The SEC is out there supposedly making sure we get full disclosure on the companies in which we are thinking of investing. It seems there ought to be more information and transparency when it comes to the past performance, outlook and strategic plans for the communities in which we are investing.

As the science improves around the movement of people and the psychology of their decisions, we will all need to pay close attention. We can't take them for granted any more. The big lesson here is that communities are a lot more important to us now. The bottom line is that we are going to need to know more about our communities, how they work and their futures. We need new predictive data to be collected and published if we are to make intelligent work out of the most important decision of our lives: where we choose to live.

Chapter 5

The Nature of Communities

If the communities we live in are the most important factor driving our happiness now, and the risk that we might live in a place that is going to go into a spiral is about to increase by an order of magnitude, then we should spend a lot more time thinking about how communities work and what factors might predict who the winners and losers will be.

To that end, I want to introduce some concepts in this chapter that I've found to be essential to constructive thinking about communities.

Think about your community as if it were a person. Communities have many of the same attributes that individuals have. Most of us have invested more time trying to figure why people are the way they are than we have thought about what makes our communities tick.

So use your acquired knowledge and insights about what makes you and what you know about what makes us so different from others, and yet so similar, to advance your thinking about communities.

Thinking about your community as if it were a person is not just a good shortcut for getting started. It is a powerful analogy for many aspects of communities, and a great way to exchange information with others down the road.

The next step to developing a practical understanding of the nature of communities is to admit that communities, even small ones, are too complicated to figure out. We are dealing with what science calls Autocatalytic Self-adapting Complex Systems.

These systems have two primary characteristics. They are too complicated for the human brain to understand, and they are changing too fast. There are just too many internal and external, dependent and independent variables. Autocatalytic Self-adapting Systems are in a constant state of evolution and never the same long enough to really figure out. This makes them impossible to understand or predict. In other words, they are unknowable.

The best we can do right now is work through theoretical constructs, mental models, metaphors and analogies. It's one of those things where the more you know, the more it seems you realize you don't know. But that's no reason to not try. And it doesn't mean that we are powerless.

In the end, dealing with complex systems becomes so overwhelming that we need a practical way of narrowing our thinking to a manageable number of factors that we can try to measure and manage. We may never get to the point where we can control or predict community quality, but if we try to we may develop the ability to influence their futures.

Communities are Like People

No two are alike. Each is driven by a unique combination of geography, experience, values, luck, vision and motivation. The DNA of a community is like human DNA, consisting of its location, geology, climate and size, among other things. A community's history is akin to an individual's personal history. How a community was established and developed provides important insights into what your community is and will be.

Each community has a name and distinct identity that is a combination of self-promoted image, cultural history, sports teams, universities, famous residents and such. Communities have personalities that run the gamut: boring to exciting, open and accepting, closed and aloof, proud to humble, modern and hip, and old-fashioned and traditional.

The same can be said of a community's character and values; they run from conservative to liberal and from tolerant to xenophobic. If you thought about it enough, you could probably come up with a person who epitomizes your community.

If you want to zero in on your community's personality, try choosing from the following list of community character attributes. Pick the five positive and five negative attributes you think best describe your community:

Ambitious	Lazy
Constructive	Self-destructive
Peaking	Peaked
Solid	Flakey
Hip	Old-fashioned
Growing	Stunted
Softened	Hardened
Had it easy	Had it hard
Endowed	Struggling
Independent	Dependent
Hopeful	Demoralized
Optimistic	Pessimistic
Cheerful	Whining
Well managed	Poorly managed
Well led	Poorly led
Rich	Poor
Flexible	Rigid
Powerful	Weak
Responsible	Irresponsible
Smart	Stupid
Creative	Myopic
Versatile	Limited
Conflicted	Resolute

Handsome	Ugly
Informed	Ignorant
Open	Closed
Positive	Negative
Fit	Fat
Productive	Dependent
Excelling	Under-achieving
Introspective	Oblivious
Contentious	Frivolous
Extroverted	Introverted
Diverse	Monolithic
Tolerant	Intolerant
Brave	Cowardly
Lucky	Unlucky
Outward looking	Inward looking
Welcoming	Aloof
Fun	Monotonous
Interesting	Boring
Healthy	Sick
Tough	Soft
Caring	Aloof
Friendly	Menacing
Clean	Dirty
Disciplined	Undisciplined
Frugal	Wasteful
Goal-directed	Reactive

Have others, both inside and outside the community, do the exercise and then talk about it. You will be amazed at how rich and revealing the discussion will be.

Communities are Like Your High School Graduating Class

When I went back to Seattle for my twenty-year high school reunion, what struck me was how many of the losers I expected to crash and burn had actually excelled, and vice versa. One particular classmate seemed to have a lock on success at graduation.

He came from a great family, was a National Merit Scholar, stand-out athlete and headed to an Ivy League school on a full ride. At the reunion, I found out he never made it through his first semester of college. He got drafted and came back from Vietnam using heroin.

Then there was the other guy. In every class of mine since fifth grade, I knew him pretty well. He had flunked a couple of grades and was still the dumbest guy in the class, and had worked his way from misdemeanor vandalism in elementary school, to breaking and entering by graduation. I was sure he would be doing life-without-parole before I finished college. At the reunion, he showed up as the CEO of a prominent local business, and married with three great kids.

The point is that some do very well with very little, while others, despite all the advantages, do very little. I think it is the same for communities. The same factors and forces that produce winners from the under-rated human beings, and losers from the well-endowed, are at work in communities. So even in the challenging times ahead, you shouldn't count any place out.

The extent to which a community has developed a sense of its future, an outlook on its destiny, and has chosen a direction and set goals and invested in a strategy and plan for getting there, is as important for communities as it is for individuals.

The Economic Base

In my junior year in college, I switched my major from Economics to Architecture and Planning because the math was getting too hard. Turned out I was the only one in my class that had taken any economics. I remember wondering why the Architecture and Planning professors didn't spend more time talking about economics, specifically the economic base of communities. It always seemed to me that the community's economic base had more influence on its form and character than any other factor.

I still believe it. The most important factor determining the nature of a community's character, form and destiny is the economic base. In the same way that each person has a purpose or reason to exist, every community has a reason to exist. For individuals, it can mean anything from raising healthy, kind and considerate children, to reversing global warming or curing cancer.

For communities, the reason they exist at all is their economic base. The economic base is simply all the things a community's residents do that bring new money into the local economy from the outside. Suffice it to say that if the economic base of a community ceases to exist for some reason, and cannot be replaced in a reasonable amount of time, hometown will be a ghost town. So one of the first steps in your quest to know a place should be to determine what economic activities are bringing in the new money. There are ten common economic base categories that make up local economic base activity:

1. Extractive industries – mining, oil and gas
2. Agriculture
3. Energy production – electric power plants
4. Federal government – including military bases and welfare transfer payments

5. State government – capitols, prisons and administrative offices
6. Educational institutions – universities
7. Tourism and hospitality for outsiders
8. Manufacturing
9. Retirees
10. Exported services

Most communities have multiple sectors to their economic base. What kind of economic base industries a community has, how diversified they are, how much they pay, and what kind of real estate and infrastructure they need all have a profound impact on a community's quality and character. That's why towns with economies based on wheat farming look and feel so much different than ones based on manufacturing or mining. If the economic base of your community is going to go through dramatic changes in the next ten years, then the nature of the community is likely to change dramatically too.

Communities are Complex Systems

Obviously, the economic base is only part of a full picture. Like individuals, communities are constantly changing. They may look the same every time you drive through, but they are changing all the time. The sheer complexity and the constant evolution of communities are two of the most important facts of their nature. And while the level of complexity is awesome, it is also intimidating and demoralizing. In fact, I think you can explain much of what is going on in a community by looking at the interaction of three critical complex systems: 1. **The Ecosystem**, 2. **The Social System**, and 3. **The Economic System**, or the three P's: Planet, People, and Payroll. When it comes to the future of communities, no system has primacy over any other. They are equal in value and importance.

The **Ecosystem** is crucial for obvious reasons. If you pollute your groundwater, your people get sick and die and the place becomes essentially uninhabitable. If you run out of water, or the bees stop pollinating your cash crop, it makes it impossible to sustain your economic base, and your community loses its reason to exist. So a neglected and degrading ecosystem will eventually unwind everything. Everyone knows that already.

The same goes for the **Social System**. I'm lumping in everything that has to do directly with the care for individual human beings into this system, that is, those not specifically central to the Eco or Economic Systems. Yes, I know you can't separate people from them. But stay with me on this. Anyone who spends most of their time working on, or worrying about the education, health of human beings or justice or their social or spiritual welfare, I consider to be working in the Social System.

If the Social System breaks down, it eventually unravels the economy. If people in a community are not healthy, if they don't get educated and trained, they can't work. If there is not enough social equity, and one segment of the population continues to win at the expense of another, then the have-nots eventually quit and bring down the whole community.

The **Economic System** is just as important. Those of us who work and worry about how to meet payrolls, manage our public institutions and earn returns on our 401(k)s, are working in the Economic System.

The Basis for Civic Morality

The way I look at it, it's the caring for these three equally important and mutually-dependent systems that is the basis for civic morality. If one system fails, the others degrade and the community degrades. The tensions created when these systems compete for a community's finite resources cause much of the conflict that both enables and confounds a community's attempts to get its act together.

If you think about it, most of the politically active people in a community can be described as caring for and advocating for one of these three areas of civic concern. The people who are trying to save the planet by stopping deforestation, preserving species, promoting water conservation, recycling and LEED (Leadership in Energy and Environmental Design) buildings are doing admirable work, and their success may well be crucial to our survival. However, they often end up faced-off with a champion of one of the other systems. And vice versa.

Passion and frustration can quickly turn conviction into extremism. People who think their cause (complex system) trumps those of others can be destructive. I've noticed that some of the fiercest ecosystem champions prefer animals to people. If they don't like people, they aren't going to care about communities. Some would just as soon see the global economy collapse and our communities fall into anarchy so the ecosystem can repair itself. So when it comes to your community, extremism in the defense of your cause is actually a vice. Acknowledging that communities are too complicated for anyone to figure out, and that these competing systems are at play will be helpful later when you have to get everyone to see they are all in the same life raft.

The Five Essentials of Community Quality

Early in my economic development career I was part of an informal group of friends and colleagues that met on and off at each other's homes to debate what factors and forces were essential to driving the quality, pace and development of the community. The core group included the city's planning director, principal of the local junior high school, senior site manager of the local Intel plant, and me, the director of economic development for the community's master developer.

In addition to vetting the local issues of the day, we engaged in a fairly serious intellectual initiative to see if we could come up with a short list of absolutes that drive the quality of a community. To make the list, the factors had to be essential, mutually-dependent, measurable and universal. To be considered "essential," we had to agree that it was crucial to maintaining the quality of a place. If a community could theoretically continue improving if the factor was unsatisfactory and getting worse, then we left it out.

Of course, if one were going to determine if the factor was satisfactory or not, you would need to be able to measure it objectively over time. Mutually-dependent meant that if the factor were to decline or degrade for an extended period of time it would eventually cause the other factors to degrade. To be considered universally essential it would have to apply to any community. Oh yeah, and we had to have unanimous agreement. Occasionally we would bring in an outside expert to try and muscle a holdout, but it never worked. After twelve years we had agreement on only five. We couldn't quite get unanimity on the sixth.

The Five Essentials of Community Quality

1. The ecosystem is stable and improving
2. World-class public education and improving
3. Low crime and improving
4. Affordable housing and improving
5. The economy is growing faster than the population

We have already talked about how the **ecosystem** can wreck a community. **Crime** will do it too. Property and violent crimes against people scare away talent and investment and makes communities build prisons and hire police instead of schools and teachers.

We considered public corruption and white-collar crime to be equally as harmful. It means the local economic and social systems are rigged against you and there is no telling what they are doing to the environment.

World-class public education is essential for a bunch of reasons. By now I shouldn't even have to even mention this one. If you don't have world-class elementary and high schools, community colleges and universities, and you are not getting most of your kids through, you will find it increasingly difficult to staff your local economy. Educated citizens commit fewer crimes, save more money, own their own homes and are more inclined to invest in improving the environment.

Affordable housing is crucial because people that own homes are better employees, build more net worth, invest more in education, commit fewer crimes, and care more about the environment. When housing costs inflate faster than wages, the increased monthly mortgage payments act like a surcharge on local labor rates and make it difficult for local economic base employers to compete with their out-of-state market rivals.

When **the economy** fails to grow faster than the population, the community loses its ability to finance and maintain infrastructure for housing and business, fund schools, fight crime and protect the environment. When tax revenues grow slower than the demand for public services, the discretionary revenue needed to improve the community dries up.

Health care was the factor we got closest to adding to the list. Transportation was a serious candidate for a while too. In practice, there is a long list of factors such as the lack of bandwidth or adequate sewage treatment capacity that can keep a community from growing its economy or attracting and keeping the workers it needs. The bottom line is that in a complex system like your community, if you lose ground on any of these essential factors through more than two election cycles, you have a problem. To figure it out you have to know how your economy really works.

Chapter 6

The New Economic Development Equation
How Economies Work
E > P

A few years ago former New Mexico Governor Bruce King asked me one of the toughest questions I had ever been asked. He had been governor three times on and off over twenty-five years and was thinking about running for one last term. He dropped by my office one day unannounced. When I asked him if he had made up his mind yet about running, he said he was still thinking about it and asked me, "If I do get to be governor again, and I can do one thing that would change the economic development future of our state, what would it be?"

As I launched into my wish list, he stopped me, held up an index finger and said, "I've heard that list, I want to know what your one thing is."

After a few seconds he realized I was going to have to think about it. He got up and headed for the door. "Call me when you get it down to one," he said.

If he asked me that question today I think my answer would surprise him. The one thing I would do to improve my state's economic development situation would be to actually define and measure economic development.

The worst thing about working in the field of economic development is attending economic development meetings. Most of these meetings are an excruciating waste of time. In fact, most of the people who really need to be there won't even go anymore, and if they do, they don't stay. When the meeting organizers start the program with "Let's go around the room and have everyone tell us their definition of economic development," make any excuse to leave.

Instead of clarifying and narrowing the agenda to get consensus for a course of action, the agenda is going to get wider and less focused, and most participants are going to leave more confused about economic development and further away from collective action than they were when they went in.

The same is true of ninety percent of community economic development strategic plans. The overwhelming majority are a complete waste of time and money, being neither strategic nor a plan. They rarely provide the reader with any insight into the way the local economy works or the community's choices. They almost never say what needs to be done, who will do it or who will pay for it.

The term "economic development" has been so overused and abused that it has lost most of its practical meaning. It's like someone said about porn: you can't define it, but you know it when you see it. This may seem like a frivolous point, but if you don't define economic development and specify the jurisdiction, your discussion will quickly devolve into "bar talk" where opinions get presented as facts, and conviction trumps logic. In the end, nothing gets settled and no one remembers anything the next morning.

I think this lack of a definition and a process for thinking about and measuring economic development will be the undoing of the economic development profession.

On the other hand, if you can develop a coherent definition and get everyone in the community to use the same mental model, same words and same data when deliberating the community's economic future, the result can be transformational. In fact, I would say it's the single most important common denominator of communities that do economic development well year after year.

Without a functional definition, even if it seems a little dictatorial to some people, and without a formal process to discipline deliberations on the subject, the effort is likely to be futile. Then you'll be putting it on your community's leaders to spend their valuable time trying to come up with a definition.

Operational Definition of Economic Development

Here's a description of the mental model I've used the past twenty-five years to define economic development. Economic development is about growing your economy faster than your population, or E > P. E is the economy, and P is the population. If you don't get anything else from this book, remember this equation:

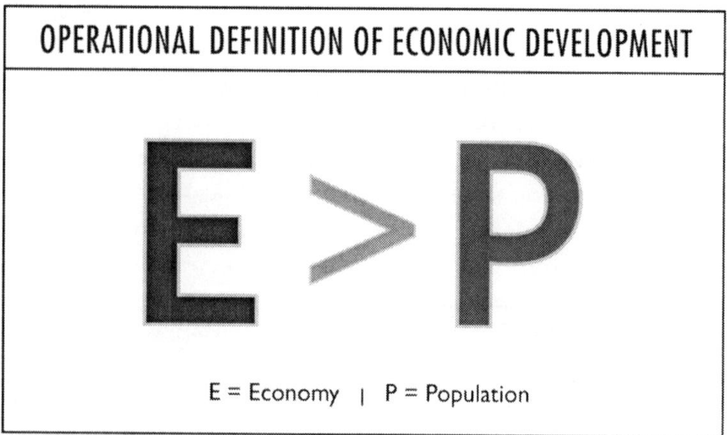

The Consequences

Economic development is about acting to ensure that the economy of your community or region (income and savings) grows faster than your population (service burden or expenses) so you have the extra resources in the future to finance improvement.

The equation applies whether your community's population is growing, shrinking, or stable. Any community where the economy is growing faster than the population, or the economy is shrinking slower than the population, will have more revenue per person to serve every year. In these cases, local households, businesses, charities, school districts, municipalities, counties and hospitals should have more revenue per person to serve than they had the year before. Over time, everyone in town should have the additional discretionary resources needed to make things better.

Any community where the economy grows slower than the population for an extended period of time faces the bleak prospect of having to serve more people each year with less revenue. If you are a private business or household, serving more people with less means you go out of business. Local tax-dependent public institutions don't go out of business. When they have to do more with less, they cut services, defer maintenance, and/or raise taxes. They also can ask the federal government to print some more money and send it to them, but that creates inflation, which is the worst kind of tax.

Our demographics make it crucial now to have a mental model about how community economies work that includes the key population factors. Half the factors driving economic development today are inherent to the community's demographics. Any approach that omits what is happening to key population factors will show only half the picture.

Implied in the phrase "economic development" is that it changes and improves an economy. If an economy grows or shrinks, but doesn't really provide the community and its institutions the ability to improve, it can't really be called development. I know that sounds like splitting hairs, but this distinction is real. The mere fact that your economy grew last year does not mean you are better off. You are only better off if the economy grew faster than your population.

It's easy to gauge the progress of your local economy by looking at three factors or metrics: 1. Economic Base, 2. Service Sector, and 3. Net Worth of resident households, businesses and institutions.

Measuring economic base activity tells you how much new money is coming into the economy. The service sector tells you how much of that income is being spent, and net worth tells you how much wealth has been created or lost. Combined, these factors show how fast your community's economy is growing.

Economic Base Jobs—The Community's Income

Economic base jobs are also referred to as export-based jobs, primary jobs, or community-income-producing jobs. Economic base jobs are those where the products and services produced by local residents are sold outside the community, bringing new money into the local economy. Traditional economic base employment sectors include tourism, agriculture, mining, oil and gas, and manufacturing, since the overwhelming majority of the products and services produced are sold to customers outside the local economy. Other sectors that can be counted as economic base include federal government employment like a military base, a national laboratory, or a regional Drug Enforcement Administration headquarters—to the extent that it is more federal employment than the community's proportional share of the national budget.

Other economic base activities are power generation beyond what is sold locally, out-of-state retirees, export services like a customer service center, and federal transfer payments such as welfare payments to the poor, disabled or unemployed—again, as long as they represent a net transfer of money from out-of-state taxpayers into the community. Do not overlook those workers that are self-employed, or free-agent workers that work out of their homes and bill out-of-state clients or employers.

These economic base, or export jobs are the ones states and communities fight to attract and keep. They are the jobs at which most of the tax incentives and training program subsidies are aimed. As long as the economic base of your community's economy is growing faster than your population, the other two metrics—the service sector and net worth—should grow. Here's another way to put it: *without an economic base, your community has no economic reason to exist.*

Service Sector—How Much is Being Spent Locally

Non-economic base jobs are called secondary jobs, local service sector, or tertiary jobs. These are jobs in which local residents produce goods and services that are sold primarily to their fellow residents in the community. These jobs are important because they produce most of the community's taxable transactions. Virtually every dime of local tax revenue is generated by private sector transactions. Local government doesn't tax itself.

The number of service sector jobs a community should have will vary depending on the size of the population, because that's what determines the number of people that need services, and the amount of money the economic base brings in. Service sector jobs usually make up a majority of the total number of jobs in a community.

The number and nature of these service sector jobs profoundly affects how long the money brought into the community by economic base employers circulates in the local economy, and how much goes into the local tax base, businesses, institutions and households.

Communities that lack a complete spectrum of retail and commercial services send local residents out of town to spend the community's economic base money. This is called Leakage. When businesses or residents buy their cars outside the community because they don't have a local dealership, then the money brought in by the community's economic base employers leaks out to a neighboring community that has one.

Adding jobs in the service sector only helps grow the economy if those jobs are producing goods and services that the community otherwise would have to buy from out of town. Adding more fast food restaurants, for example, rarely helps grow the economy or stop someone from going out of town to eat. It merely divides the community's fast food market into smaller slices of the economic pie. Otherwise, you could solve all of your employment problems by opening up a hundred new fast food restaurants every year.

It would be different, though, if a community had no general merchandiser, forcing local residents to go to a neighboring community to do their shopping. Then recruiting a Target, K-Mart or Wal-Mart would make the local economy bigger without necessarily increasing the economic base. Before the city I lived in, Rio Rancho, New Mexico, had its first general merchandiser, if I had a list of ten things I had to shop for on Saturday mornings, and if there was one thing on the list I couldn't get locally, I would end up going into Albuquerque and getting everything. After a K-Mart opened in Rio Rancho, I found myself heading into Albuquerque once a month instead of once a week. Other residents did the same, and Rio Rancho saw a surge in gross receipts tax revenue.

Mesa del Sol Metrics

In 2004, I started a consulting assignment for FCE Covington, a partnership of two of the most creative and prolific master-planned community developers in the country. The land they were bidding on was part of an extensive portfolio of bulk land held in trust by the New Mexico State Land Office. The land had been owned by the state since statehood and was now enveloped by the city of Albuquerque. The 15,000-plus contiguous acres was the largest contiguous piece of undeveloped infill property in the U.S. Aside from being the most valuable piece of land in the state land trust, the tract was the last major chunk of undeveloped land in Albuquerque's city limits. It was the most strategic piece of land left to develop.

Forest City Enterprises was ten years into a landmark project that was being developed on the site of Denver's old Stapleton Airport. It was eying an even bigger, more ambitious project 444 miles south on I-25 in Albuquerque, called Mesa del Sol.

I was hired by the company's chairman Albert Ratner to craft an economic development strategy that would guarantee the city, state and the development community that the project would create the economy needed to support the new residential population, and that it would not be built on the backs of existing taxpayers.

To that end, we promised to create the new jobs required to support the 100,000 new residents planned for the site. I think we were the first developer in the country to agree that as a part of our development agreements with the city and state that we would create twice as many economic base jobs as we needed to support the new residents.

This is how the math worked: 100,000 new residents and 38,000 new residential units. At build-out it would be the second largest city in New Mexico.

For 100,000 new people, we would need roughly 50,000 jobs. At that time, forty-seven percent of the state's population was in the workforce. Using economic base theory, we figured that that a city of Albuquerque's size would need to first create 15,000 new economic base jobs to get 50,000 new jobs.

Those 15,000 economic base jobs would in turn cause 35,000 new service sector jobs to be created over the next three years. To remove any concerns that our development would take market share from other parts of the city or divert exiting tax revenue, we committed to create twice the number of economic base jobs we would need, or 30,000 new economic base jobs.

To count as economic base jobs (we would not count service sector jobs), they would have to be full-time, and the employer would have to demonstrate that over sixty-five percent of their products and services were sold out of state. The jobs would have to pay above the median income in the economic base, an average of $45,000 to $50,000 a year.

They would have to be new to the city. In other words, they would not count if the employer merely moved from another part of the city.

And the total number of economic base jobs would have to be in place proportionally ahead of any new housing starts. It worked out to 0.8 economic base jobs per residential unit. The developer's goal was to build 600 new homes a year, which meant we would have to create 474 net new economic base jobs every year.

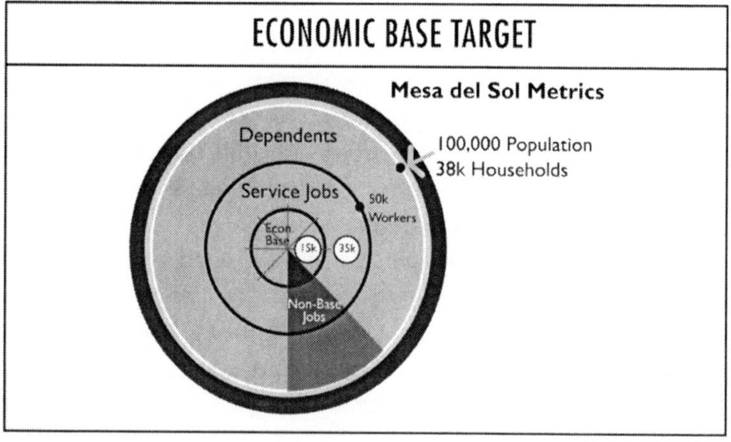

This approach demonstrates how to think about how many jobs you will need to sustain the population you project to have. But how rich the community already is can be a major mitigating factor, and needs to be part of the calculations of how your local economy works.

Net Worth

Communities that are relatively poor and getting poorer are much more vulnerable to the business cycle and the looming labor supply problems. How much of the community's economic base income is actually staying on the balance sheets of resident businesses and households is a good thing to know. Tracking local net worth will help you account for the value your retired residents have on the community's economy.

The biggest component of resident net worth is usually the value of people's homes. If home values are appreciating faster than inflation, your residents are building net worth on top of any savings they have. So factors like the ratios of home ownership to renters, stick-built to mobile homes, and the age and condition of the local housing stock are important indicators of a community's net worth and the direction in which it is headed. Of course, premium-driven inflation in housing values—where land and home values rise wildly because of more demand than supply—feel good on the way up, but they aren't real if they rise on a bubble.

The ultimate effect of rising home values is new equity created on local residents' balance sheets. This has three positive impacts on a community's economy. It gives people more money to spend, which improves revenue per square foot in local retail and commercial businesses, and raises property values and sales tax revenues. It increases residential property tax value, meaning tax revenues. And it creates the net worth needed for retirement, which is important for surviving the coming surge in Boomer retirees. If the retirees are poor or run out of net worth half way through their golden years, the community is going to be in trouble.

The extent to which your retired residents, or those near retirement, have suffered net worth losses in their 401(k)s, or lost equity in their homes, is another factor that will impact the economy side of the equation. Whether the net worth gained by residents is earned, or came as a windfall, the effect is the same. The economy side of the equation gets bigger.

Rio Rancho

During the twelve years I was doing economic development for the community of Rio Rancho, the Intel Corporation invested $16 billion and developed 3 million square feet of microchip manufacturing facilities and hired over 5,000 employees. Since all the computer chips manufactured in the Rio Rancho facility were purchased by out-of-state customers, the money the plant paid out in salaries came from outside the community and made the local economic base and economy bigger. When 100 new hires got their first paychecks and started spending it, the community's service sector employers suddenly got more business.

As new employees went out into the community with their paychecks, they went to the local bank to open accounts and deposit their checks. Then they might have dropped off their cars at Leonard Tire to get their tires rotated. Then they walked over to 4B's Restaurant for lunch, and on the way back to the plant, they stopped by Walgreens to get batteries for their calculators, or some Tylenol.

So Ron Smith at United New Mexico Bank had to hire a new account representative and an additional teller. Don Leonard had to hire an extra tire buster. Steve Kennedy at 4B's had to hire another cook and another waitress. Noble Sysco, their food supply company, had to buy another delivery truck and hire another driver, and Walgreens had to staff an additional register and hire an additional inventory auditor.

Eventually, as more people were hired at the plant, new banks, tire stores and restaurants had to be built and staffed. In the meantime, the community's tax base expanded as increasing retail and commercial transactions drove up sales tax revenue. As the number of local commercial businesses increased and store sales increased, property values in the city's tax base grew. The city's commercial tax revenue streams grew faster than its residential tax base for the next twenty years, and provided all local tax-dependent institutions a little more money per person to serve each year. The commercial tax base grew faster than the residential tax base. During the next twelve years, household income grew from $19,000 a year to $44,000, and land values (property tax valuations), appreciated dramatically. Commercial property values rose from $3.50 a square foot to $12.

With the increased revenue, Rio Rancho was able to begin controlling its own destiny. Within a decade, the city went from being a destitute bedroom community of starter homes ridiculed by Albuquerque residents for the lack of local services and substandard schools, to one of the most progressive and desirable places in the region to live. In the process, Rio Rancho residents and business owners saw the quality of their lives improve and their net worth increase dramatically.

Since 2000, Rio Rancho has lost ground as Intel downsized its plant. New home building continued for retiring Californians, and the residential service burden began to outpace local job creation. That put the city behind the eight-ball again. Sometimes community leaders mistake local tax receipt increases as proof they are getting richer, when in reality they are adding municipal and county service burdens faster than the tax base can support them after the construction slows or stops. But Rio Rancho is one of the few communities in the country that measures its economic base. It has one of the best economic development programs in the country, and its leaders understand what is happening.

Economic Expansion vs. Economic Development vs. Economic Improvement Growth for Growth's Sake

Economic expansion doesn't necessarily mean everyone in the community is better off. There are scenarios where the economy can grow substantially, but the community actually gets poorer. Economic expansion may occur because the population grew substantially that year. But the economy has to grow faster than the population for the community to improve. This may seem like splitting hairs, but not all growth is improvement. New gross receipts taxes, fees, income and assessed valuation are all generated by the building of new houses. The problem is that the construction of a new home is a one-time event. It's not sustainable. Each new household creates additional ongoing service burdens and infrastructure maintenance costs roughly equal to the tax revenue it generates.

A community like Prescott, Arizona, for example, must be careful not to be lulled into a false sense of economic security by new home construction and a new Wal-Mart. It'll have to serve these people with police and fire protection after housing slows down and construction revenue dries up. Sure, the new residents pay property taxes, but they aren't bringing new, outside money into the community. Pretty soon, their property and sales taxes won't be enough to pay for the police and fire coverage they need. That'll overwhelm the community's resources.

Mobile Home Scenario

If your community has a high percentage of households in mobile or modular homes that will depreciate faster than their mortgages, you could be overestimating the value of your economy.

Retiree Scenario

Retirees can be good and bad for a community. In places like Sun City, Arizona, where they *are* the community, you could look at new retirees coming into the community bringing the money and government entitlements they earned on their jobs in other parts of the country as a source of new economic base income. But if the new retirees are poorer than the average household in your community, it will not help. In fact, you will probably get poorer. Communities should be careful when thinking of attracting retirees as an economic development strategy. Too many retirees, and too many poor ones, can result in public services being swamped and school bond issues being voted down. As long as they are bringing in more than they are taking, and they are making the place better, you're okay.

Tourism and Hospitality

The tourism and hospitality industry is the primary economic base sector for many rural communities, and is turning out to be an important sector in most. It is also one where a good chamber of commerce or community events promotion programs can actually create new economic base income for the community by coming up with events like jazz festivals, art shows and sporting events.

In my first economic development job in Grants, New Mexico, I knew that it was going to take eighteen months or longer to bring in the first new employer, and I wanted to make an immediate contribution. I noticed that some of my old college swimming buddies who were doing triathlons didn't have any events in the winter, so we came up with a fifty-mile bike, run, cross-country ski and snowshoe race from the town of Grants to the top of 11,000-foot-high Mt. Taylor and back. We called it the Mt. Taylor Quadrathlon. Since 1984, the event has been packing the local motels and restaurants with a thousand plus visitors every Presidents' Day weekend.

But the downside of tourism and hospitality can be the relatively low wages that are paid to most hospitality workers. So it's one of those economic base sectors where it may look like you are adding new jobs and increasing tax revenue some years, but you could be adding to the service burden faster.

Many tourism-driven economies, like ones with ski areas, are vulnerable to feast-or-famine cycles depending on how much snow falls or the price of gas.

Casino Gaming

Casino gaming is economic development for a community if most of the people gambling there are visiting from outside the area. But if the majority of the casino's patrons are local residents stopping on their way home on payday, it is not. If most of the customers are locals, then you could look at gaming as a tax on your neighbors who are really bad at math. For a Native American community with a casino on the outskirts of a metro area or on a major highway, it can be a spectacular economic base generator as it transfers major amounts of wealth every year from people outside their communities.

U.S.-Mexico Border Scenarios

Another false scenario is the case of unbalanced immigration. The five poorest communities in the U.S. are on the U.S.-Mexico border. Except for San Diego, border towns are poor and have been losing ground against the rest of the nation because their economic base is primarily the warehousing industry serving the value-added manufacturing industries across the border in Mexico. Many of the sub-components that are exported to the Mexican maquilas for assembly are warehoused in U.S. distribution centers on the border. Finished products are shipped back to U.S. border warehouses for sorting, packaging and distribution. The problem for these warehousing-based economies is that forklift drivers don't make a lot of money to begin with, and compared to other types of value-added work, you can't drive a forklift a lot better after two years, so your wages don't go up.

On the population side of the equation, these communities have been getting buried in new poor, uneducated residents every year. In some ways, our border towns are examples of what many places are going to be dealing with when they hit Catastrophic Full Employment: their economies are growing slower than their populations: E < P.

Potential False Negative Scenarios

Potential "False negative" scenarios are situations where something that looks bad might actually turn out to be good, or at least have a major mitigating affect.

1. Contraction scenarios
2. Possible opportunities
3. Snowbirds
4. Company closing – industry leaving
5. Housing values go up too fast
6. Housing values go down

Confusing economic expansion—whether driven by population growth or windfall economic events like spiking corn prices—with lasting economic development is one of the reasons so many people have become cynical and suspicious of the economic development mantra of big business, government, and real estate developers. Growing the economy by growing the population is a magic trick, or better yet, a vanishing act, because when the economic activity disappears, the city's obligations don't. This has caused "economic development" to become code words for accelerating population growth, to be condemned by environmentalists and cheered by the business community, which mistakenly believes that a broader customer base is all they need to prosper. They'd see things differently if they'd learn to look at the local economy by asking two vital questions. First, how does the economy generate income? And how well does it retain income? To understand the difference, it's time to turn to **Economic Base Theory**. It's the basis for lasting economic development, and unlike residential construction-based economies, it pays dividends for years to come.

For example, think about what inflation does to the GDP. If from one year to the next, bread, milk and eggs cost more than they used to, and your dry cleaning bills go up, and your accountant wants more money to do your taxes, and local factories have to pay more for their raw materials, your community's gross product will rise even though its economic activity hasn't. Local economies driven by housing starts are another example of the way numbers can distort the true nature of a local economy. My second job as an economic developer in Rio Rancho depended on solving just such a problem.

In the end, there are really only two ways that your community can hope to end up a little richer: manage the development of the economy and/or manage the development of the population.

The Economy Side of E > P

There are only three ways to grow the economy side of the equation: grow the economic base, stop leakage, or increase local net worth. Here's a list of the ways this can be done.

Growing the economy can only occur three ways:

1. Grow the economic base and/or
2. Grow the service sector (reduce leakage)
3. Increase net worth

Growing the economic base only happens six ways:

1. Increase the total number of economic base jobs
2. Growth of high-value economic base sectors and/or attrition of low-value sectors
3. Increased productivity of your economic base workers increases wages

4. Increase the number of wealthy retirees
5. Increase the value of government transfer payments
6. Wait for windfall events like spikes in uranium and natural gas prices

Expanding the service sector only happens four ways:

1. Increase the range of goods and services offered
2. Increase the quality of goods and services
3. Reduce the costs (prices) of local services & cost of living
4. Increase the productivity of service sector workers

Increasing net worth only happens four ways:

1. Raise rate of home ownership
2. Raise home value & appreciation
3. Windfall investment returns
4. Raise value of locally owned assets

Economic development efforts used to be able to succeed by executing a strategy to grow the economic base a little each year. It's clear now that seismic changes in the nature of the economy and our demographics have rendered many traditional approaches ineffective. But that doesn't mean we should give up. We are going to need to innovate and look for new ways to manage E > P. It's also clear that we will have to start looking seriously at the population side of the equation for solutions.

Chapter 7

The Population Side of E > P
The Weak-side Shift and the Assent of the Workforce

For most of human history, population has been the strong side of the E > P equation. My father's generation and the generations before his had between four and twelve kids. That was two to six times the number needed to replace themselves, so each generation coming into the workforce was much bigger in proportion to the existing economy. The field of economic development is in large part the civic response of community leaders to the chronic oversupply of new workers. I think one of the reasons it's so difficult for people to see labor shortage forecasts as a problem is that it runs counter to thousands of years of the human experience of having large families. Our brains may even have some prehistoric hardwiring that presumes our species will continue producing more workers than we need.

If anything reinforced this assumption, it was the glut of 78 million Baby Boomers that came of working age in the 1960s and 1970s. Boomers flooded virtually every local job market with way more qualified workers than the economy could absorb. The pressure on local leaders to create jobs was so great, and the presumption of oversupply so ingrained in our thinking, that the population side of the equation was taken for granted or even discarded. There was always plenty of labor, but never enough jobs. In the U.S., where we have seen ourselves as the Promised Land with hordes of people from other parts of the world begging to come here to work, the idea that we could run out of labor just doesn't compute.

One effect of this perpetual oversupply presumption is that concern for the population side of the equation is secondary. Not to say we didn't acknowledge the importance of health, education and social equity, but it was too easy to subordinate them to the more immediate and concrete threat of not having enough jobs. In fact, joblessness was seen in large part as the cause of our community's health, education and social justice problems.

As I said before, when you saw the family across the street failing to get their kids to school prepared to learn and allowing them to underperform and eventually drop out, it was sad from a humanitarian standpoint. But be honest, in the back of your mind you thought, if they didn't have enough sense to stay in school and get an education, there would be less competition for your kids.

Concern for the population side of the equation was rooted in a sense of humanitarian concern and general appreciation that a well-educated population was good for the country. It was not considered the biggest threat to our economy or national security. The unemployment rate and the Russians were.

In the mid 1990s, when the U.S. started to reach full employment, and shortages in some career fields started appearing, we saw the first signs of weakness on the population side. It was the late 1980s and early 1990s when the Boomers became *the* economy and the smaller generations coming behind them could not oversupply the economy to the same degree. Obviously, there were a lot of other structural economic factors at work too, but we first started seeing unemployment rates in many communities under four percent.

I can remember when six percent was considered structural full employment and thought to be unattainable.

The central point of this book is that we are witnessing a strong-side/weak-side shift in the economic development equation. Creating new jobs by jacking up the economy was the solution when the economy was the weak side of E > P. Full employment and chronic shortages of qualified workers in the years ahead will turn the tables. Instead of not enough jobs, it will be not enough workers, or more accurately, not enough qualified workers.

Population is now the weak side. With a chronic shortage of qualified labor, the focus must shift. Now we must solve it from the population side. The economy is still important. I'm not suggesting you dismantle your economic development programs or demote the importance of the economy. It just means that the game must shift from a singular focus on job creation to a much more complicated and difficult focus on workforce creation.

Total Population

In this chapter I am going to try and describe the mental model I use to explain how the dynamics of the population side of the equation affect economic improvement. One problem I need to tell you about up front is that, because we haven't considered it important until now, we don't know much about this side of the equation. And don't let labor economists and demographers tell you they can get the data you need to understand your workforce predicament. They can't. We don't collect it. The biggest problem might be that we don't have a practical mental model for thinking about the population side of the equation. We can figure out what new data we need, and how to get it, down the road.

The best way I've found to visualize the population side of the equation at the community level is to think of two contrasting pie charts. The first describes your population today, the other, your population in ten years. If your population is bigger in ten years, the future population pie chart will be proportionally bigger. You could also use the increased size of the future population to represent the need for a bigger economy. How big your economy will need to be depends on how many people it has to support. The number of jobs available in a community tends to scale to the size of the population because everyone needs transportation, medical care, groceries, home repair, financial services, insurance, etc. So projecting total future population is an important first step.

This is harder than it sounds, especially considering that most community leaders don't like to talk about population growth predictions. First, it means they have to set aside more resources for future infrastructure and services, and as a result, have less to spend on their constituents in the current election cycle. This is true whether the population is going to grow or shrink. Second, their constituents, especially the no-growth factions, tend to associate talking about population growth with promoting or causing it. As a result, most communities dramatically underestimate population growth and try to avoid the subject altogether. If you poke around, though, you can probably find that planner or demographer in the bowels of the city or county that really knows what is going on. Just don't ask them to go on the record.

The Inverted Dependency Ratio

So once you have the size of your population pegged, the next thing you need to know is the ratio of dependent-aged residents to working-age residents. This is called the dependency ratio. Today, that ratio is pretty even in most communities. But it is not going to stay that way. The proportions of dependents—those too old, too young or physically incapable of working (dependents)—to the proportion of residents of working age and able to work is going to invert and grow increasingly imbalanced in the next ten to twenty years.

In the graphic below, the population of the community is growing and causing the economy to need to grow. The problem is that the community's most experienced and productive workers are retiring and becoming dependents faster than new qualified workers are being educated and trained to replace them. At some point after full employment, the community will no longer have enough qualified workers to staff the economy.

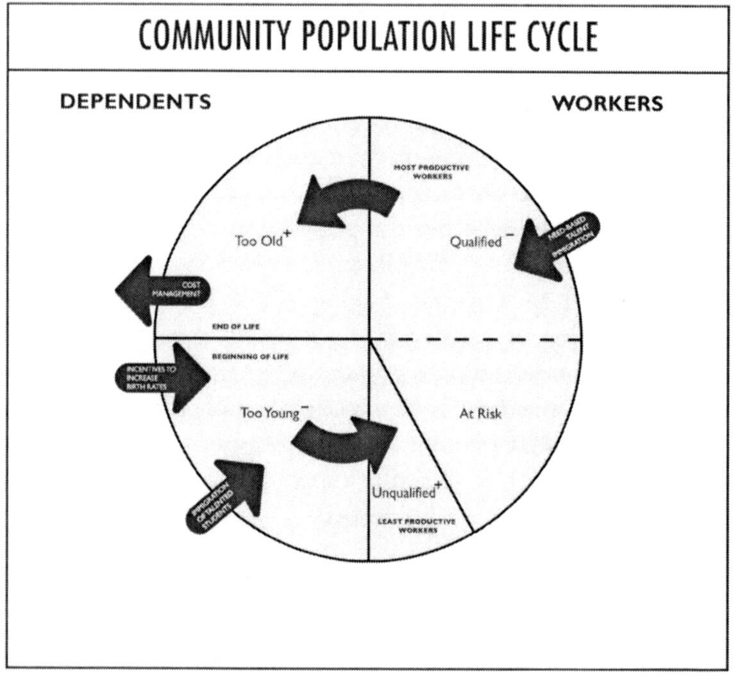

An inverted dependency ratio means that the number of people in the community who are of working age is smaller in proportion to the number of people who can't or won't work. So, as you look at the pie chart of the population today, it's balanced. Roughly half the residents are dependents.

Ten years from now the population pie will not only be bigger, but the dependents will have increased in proportion to workers. This basically shows the impact of workers retiring and becoming dependents faster than young dependents are getting educated and becoming workers.

This only describes part of the problem. To see the truly scary part of the jam we are in, you need to look at dependents and workers just a little bit deeper.

To do this, think of the population as consisting of four quadrants, two on the dependent side and two on the worker side. On the dependent side there are those too old to work and those too young to work.

On the worker side there are those qualified to work and those unqualified. For the purpose of this discussion, let's define unqualified to be anyone earning less than 1.5 times the poverty rate—or those without the education, skills and experience to earn 1.5 times the poverty rate.

So now, looking at your population pie, starting at twelve o'clock and going clockwise down the worker side, you have a gradient starting with the oldest workers, the closest to retirement, the most experienced, the most productive, and some would say, the hardest working part of the workforce. As you move down around the right side of the workforce gradient, the workers get generally younger and less productive until you get to the borderline unqualified.

From there, wherever that line is, your workforce can be thought to be consuming more goods and services than they produce. Sometimes highly qualified workers find themselves pushed back into the unqualified quadrant because their industry is destroyed by technology, global competition, or a degrading business climate. Industry destruction and the resulting skills mismatch can cause a dramatic, simultaneous contraction of a community's qualified quadrant and an explosion of the unqualified sector overnight.

Moving down the unqualified quadrant to the bottom of the pie chart, the population of working-age residents grows generally younger, less capable and less motivated, until somewhere toward the bottom you cross into the quadrant of dependents that are too young to work. These would be the teenagers who are capable of working but still in school.

Continuing up the dependent side through the too-young quadrant, the population gets younger and more dependent until you reach totally dependent newborns.

At that border of the too-young-to-work quadrant and the too-old quadrant would be the newborns, and next, those at the end of life. The quadrant of the too-old has a gradient beginning with the totally dependent, oldest, most feeble and nearest to death at nine o'clock, with the retired elders getting younger and more capable, more productive and more likely to be able to work until we are back where we began—those workers ready to retire.

One of the things you want to ask yourself is whether there is a quadrant or aspect of the population that is more important than the others. The other question is whether you have any control or influence over it.

The Qualified Quadrant is the One That Counts

Stated bluntly, if your qualified quadrant doesn't grow at a faster rate than the other three, your economy won't be able to grow faster than the population.

What happens to the relative balance or proportion of these four quadrants in the next ten years is going to have a profound impact on the quality and character of your community.

Again, the problem with our future is that the quadrant we need to grow is going to shrink, and shrink fast, and the ones we need to shrink are going to explode.

The fourth quadrant (too-young-to-work) can work for you or against you. If your too-young-to-work population is growing faster than your qualified-worker sector because kids are unprepared, unable, or unwilling to stay in school, take harder classes and get ready for work, you are doomed.

If your community's too-young quadrant is growing fast because families are deciding to have more kids and they are getting them through college, you'll be okay, providing they stay or come back after graduation.

Managing Community Population

Managing the population side of the economic improvement equation is going to be tricky. First, we don't have an intellectual model that allows competing factions to see that their destinies are linked.

Second, the data needed to think about the population side issues in a concrete way doesn't exist, is going to be expensive to get, and no one wants to pay extra for bad news. Third, there are some pretty sticky ethical, moral and legal prohibitions against trying to manage populations. And we don't want to go there.

But it's safe to say that community improvement agendas are going to need to shift from pure job creation strategies to ones that manage these population quadrants.

As you use this workforce life cycle model to think of the P side of the E > P equation, you find opportunities for innovation and action on the quadrant frontiers.

The Four Frontiers—Where the Action Is

Retirement Frontier

At the top of the pie chart there is the frontier of the oldest workers ready to retire and move across to become retired dependents.

When you think about it, the largest, most productive and hardest working part of the workforce is about to bail on the economy, taking vital knowledge and experience with them.

What can we do to keep them working longer? Are there ways to incentivize them to keep working? Can neuroscience figure out how to keep older brains functioning at peak performance for longer?

Qualification Frontier

When it comes to the frontier between qualified and unqualified workers, there is a lot to think about. What's making your qualified worker sector grow? What's making it shrink? Are you educating and attracting more qualified workers every year than move out? When technology or global competition destroys or transforms one of your key employment sectors, it can mean that a big chunk of previously very qualified, highly-productive workers just became unqualified. Until and unless they get retrained, they and your community will suffer. Major industry dislocations are a little like a track official raising the bar on a high jumper after they've left the ground. The mismatch of skills to work is a huge problem that will only get worse.

The fact is, in communities with a rapidly growing unqualified-worker quadrant, whether from a major skill mismatch, industry dislocation, a broken school system, or a flood of immigrants unprepared to learn, the result will be the same. One of the biggest problems I see is that we don't even have a national standard for work readiness. There are some programs that could work, but we are still a long way away from a standard that parents, students, mid-career change candidates, educators and employers can all use.

The School-to-Work Frontier

Maybe the most important area is the school-to-work frontier. Whether you blame the high rate of divorce, racism, teachers unions, parents, secular humanism, hip-hop, gang-bangers, or greedy corporate special interests, it doesn't really matter. The public school system, by any accounting, is a disaster and only getting worse. It's way past whether we ought to use vouchers or charter schools. In fact, I think a top-to-bottom overhaul of our public school system is our most important national security issue. There is no way our country is going to be able to maintain a superpower economy if we continue to drop half our school kids in the proverbial academic dirt. With such a huge block of the population bailing out of the workforce, it is mathematically impossible to keep our economy balanced if we don't rescue the kids who are dropping through the cracks of our school system meltdown.

Procreation-Life-Expectancy Frontier

The procreation-life-expectancy frontier is important in the long-term. On the one hand, we are living a lot longer than our DNA programming intended, and personally, I'm okay with that. Maybe we Boomers will feel bad enough about not having enough kids, wrecking the school system and poisoning the planet to figure out how to check out of this life without blowing our retained earnings, and those of the country, on expensive, ultimately futile end-of-life procedures. Did you know that ninety percent of what we Americans spend on health care is spent in the last six months of our lives? Pretty stupid as a society, really.

But as a species (more accurately as industrialized countries), we are being even more stupid—suicidal actually—in not having enough offspring to replace ourselves. In fact, I think that is how you get on the endangered species list. Someone should call the Sierra Club and get things started.

But let's get back to talking about your community surviving. In the glory days of economic development it was simpler, and in a lot of ways, easier to manage the E > P equation. All we had to do was generate a few new economic base jobs every year and the community could get better. Now, economic development is as much about managing your population as it is managing your economy. Managing the population is new territory for most of us.

At this writing, I don't know of any community that's measuring and projecting the changes in their workforce and dependent sectors in a meaningful way. If your community leaders are not measuring and projecting the proportion dynamics of the too old, too young, qualified and unqualified, then they are flying blind.

Are you thinking about your community in this way? Can you populate a pie chart like this? Can everyone see what is happening? Do you know what you don't know? I'll bet not. Know that getting data for this mental model is going to be harder than you think.

There is one last thing about communities that I want to get into here, and it deserves its own chapter. And that is leadership. Going back to the notion that communities are like people, leadership is the community equivalent of gumption, that rare human trait or spirit that makes champions of underdogs, and the lack of which makes slackers out of those with all the advantages. Some places that look sure to crash and burn will make it, while others that seem to have it made will perish. As it is with people, gumption will be a trait you will want to look for in a community.

Chapter 8

Community Gumption and Leadership

Where you choose to live is now a high-stakes bet. And our demographic inertia is making the odds worse by the minute. A better analogy than gambling may be stock picking. When you pick stocks you study a mix of factors: the general direction of the industry sector, market position, capitalization and sales, among other things.

One of the most important factors in stock analysis is management, or what some call the leadership question. Who is on the board? Who is the CEO? Who are the people running key divisions of the company?

How are they chosen? What is their track record? How do they size up the market? What is their vision of the future? What is the plan? How do decisions get made? What kind of research department do they have? Do they get the things done they say they will?

Whether you are sizing up a new community to live in or evaluating the one you live in now, there are things you want to know. After all, this is going to be the place on which you bet your life. You're betting your happiness, health, net worth—a whole range of variables. You certainly don't want to pick a loser.

Can this community grow, attract and hold enough talent to staff the economy it will need? Even when the rest of the industrialized world can't because there aren't enough qualified workers to go around? Is your community one of the talent magnets, and is it doing the things it needs to do to stay one? If the community is losing talent, and the qualified worker quadrant is shrinking in proportion to the others, do local leaders know it, and are they doing anything about it? In some cases the assessment either way will be obvious. Maybe it's already evident that the place is great and getting better, or maybe it's already in an irreversible tailspin. For places considered to be "on the bubble," leadership dynamics will loom large.

Is there a history of strong, stable, visionary leadership? Are the community's leaders aware of and willing to admit what they don't know? Are they trying to get data? Do they look ahead and see what is coming? Do they have a plan? Are they making good decisions and getting things done? In most cases, it's a quick yes or no; they either do or they don't. Most don't.

I'd like to continue a little longer with the analogy that communities are like people. There is a variable that drives some of our fellow human beings to overcome terrible odds and do spectacular things. Call it will. Call it gumption. Call it inspiration. Call it the human spirit. Whatever it is, it's the great differentiator at every level of individual human endeavor. I think this same gumption factor is at work differentiating communities.

Some people think individuals have to be born with this quality, and that may partially be the case. To some extent though, it can be taught, learned or discovered. Using the right mental model with the right words, and following the right process, you can learn how to use a combination of planning and volition to make a better life, or at least greatly improve the odds that you will. If you do everything that Steven Covey says to do in his book *The 7 Habits of Highly Effective People,* your life and your influence on your future will improve. If you look closely, many of the principles and processes laid out by self-improvement gurus like Covey, Lou Tice and Tony Robbins for helping individuals are being applied to the management of successful communities.

During an eight-year stint doing economic development for Santa Teresa, a New Mexico border community, I spent most of my "give back" time working with elementary and middle schools in the nearby Colonia of Sunland Park. At the time, it was probably the poorest incorporated city in the country. Household incomes averaged less than $9,000 a year, and they were often big households. The 12,000-plus residents were almost entirely first-or second-generation Mexican immigrants. Most were more comfortable speaking Spanish at home, as well as in city council meetings and in most business transactions.

One of the school projects I tried to get started involved the development of a curriculum for teaching how to set goals, as well as motivation and performance techniques. In a previous life as a swimming coach, I spent a lot of time perfecting this process for my swimmers, parents and coaches.

Most of the process we developed was based on the early work of Lou Tice and the Pacific Institute, a performance consultancy focused mainly on improving the performance of professional athletes and professional and collegiate sports organizations. Every year I had a team of the Institute's consultants come in and provide a series of seminars for every swimmer over eleven years old, their parents and my assistant coaches. During the week-long program, we ran seminars on how the brain worked, motivation, visualization, and why goals had to be set a certain way for them to work.

Running that program every year was the single most important thing we did as a team. Everyone with a role in the program came away with three important things. It transformed the mentality of many of our swimmers and their parents. Second, it provided the team a common terminology needed to learn from and support each other.

Third, it demystified the whole idea of how to get good at something, and gave everyone a clear and simple path and a formal process that practically guarantees success. Watching this simple process transform the lives of the people in our program was more gratifying than winning state championships or getting our swimmers onto Olympic teams.

Some twenty years after I left coaching, I thought I could dust off the curriculum, teach it to some of the students and parents at my adopted schools and get the same results I'd gotten as a swimming coach.

Boy was I wrong. After a few weeks of testing it out on a small focus group, I was getting nowhere. It wasn't just one or two, it was everyone: kids, parents and teachers. They just weren't getting it.

At first I thought it might be a language problem. I had learned to speak Spanish during my Peace Corps assignment in Chile, and it was obvious that many words and phrases just don't translate from English to Spanish. I also realized that if you don't have the words and the sentence structure in your language to say something, you can't think it. Language may have been part of the problem, but something else was wrong.

I consulted the parish priest on the problem, and he suggested it was what he called the mentality of poverty. He knew the families in my group pretty well and he said most of them probably didn't believe they had any power to affect the future.

If you grow up without ever being encouraged to try and do something that you are not sure you can do, plan out the intermediate milestones, make the necessary sacrifices and investments to reach the milestones, reach the goal and celebrate it as something you helped cause, then the intellectual infrastructure for planning and investing for a future outcome is simply not there.

If by the time you are twenty you have not been around parents, siblings or peers who have been setting goals, and you have never tried it yourself, there are really only three ways you can picture becoming affluent and successful. You either inherited it, you stole it, or you won the lottery. But without a successful goal-setting experience, and the words and phrases to talk about it, the fourth way simply does not exist. Your brain doesn't have the software applications.

When I rolled up for one of my seminar sessions in my new company car and wearing nice clothes, the students and their families were sizing me up, trying to figure which of the three I was: born rich, thief, or just lucky. It never occurred to me that it never occurred to them that there was a fourth way.

You need four concrete concepts to make this work. You need the notion that you can change the future by volition, the right words, a logical process, and the imprint of some successful experience. Your peers, your family members or you yourself have to have an example of success. If any of those are missing, you may not have the intellectual infrastructure to know there is a fourth way. The inability to imagine a fourth path is an absolute barrier to personal development. I think it's a root cause of chronic poverty and hopelessness.

At some point, you can divide the world's population into two groups. You can divide the communities of the world into two groups as well. The break is between those that think they have some control or influence over how things turn out, and those that don't. If your community's leaders think they are powerless to control or influence the community's future, they are right. That belief will be self-fulfilling.

The Gumption Cycle

The ability of a person to influence their future depends on what I call the gumption cycle.

Setting out to do something you are not sure you can do takes more courage. But it takes more than that. It requires working what I call the Gumption Cycle.

The cycle begins with the concept of self-determination. **1. Believe**. Do you really believe that you as an individual, or your community as an isolated whole, have any power or influence over the way things turn out? **2. Think**. If you believe you have influence over your future, you will be much more likely to think about it. If you feel powerless, then you won't. You might spend time wishing or fretting about what might

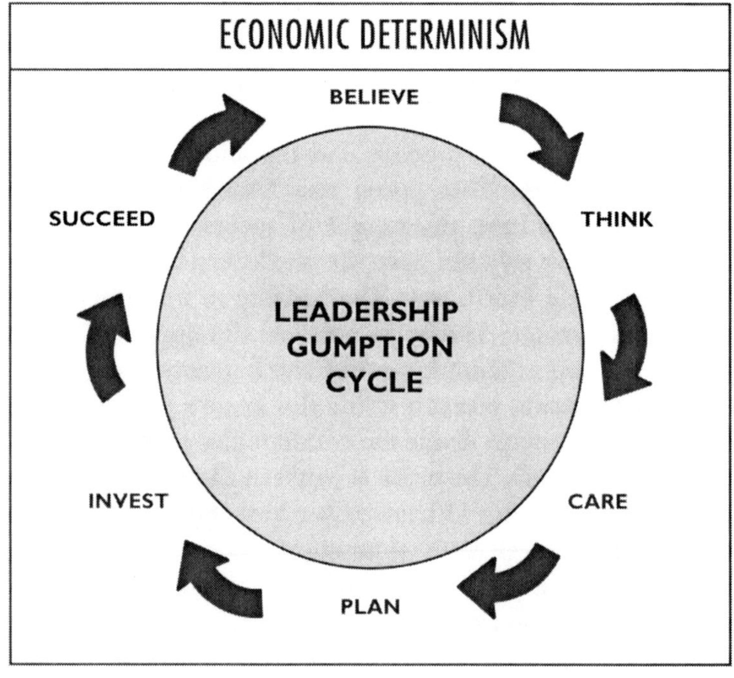

happen, but you are unlikely to invest a lot of time thinking about something you believe you have no ability to influence. **3. Care**. If you spend enough time thinking about the future, you begin to care about it. **4. Plan**. If you care about the future, you will be inclined to set goals and make a plan. And **5. Investment**. When goals are set properly and plans are made, it leads to the investment of time and resources. **6. Success and attribution**. The investment in a plan inevitably raises the probabilities that it will succeed.

When success is finally achieved, you are more inclined to attribute that success to your own volition. That reinforces your belief that you have some influence how your life turns out. The cumulative acts of believing, thinking, caring, planning, investing and succeeding give an individual a sense of power. Every time you do it, it makes you stronger, more confident and more successful.

It amazes me how energizing even the smallest act of volition in pursuit of a plan or goal can be. The degree to which a person believes in their ability to influence the future, and the processes they use to manage their discretionary resources is a major differentiator for both people and communities.

I had a young employee once who was pushing thirty, married and divorced twice, and still living with her parents. In her quarterly performance reviews I tried to get her to consider going back to school part time to pick up some additional skills and knowledge so we could start giving her more interesting work, responsibility and money. These were all results she claimed she wanted.

After three years of inaction, it became obvious that she didn't really believe she had any influence over her life. Life was happening to her. She left control of her life on the default setting you can call destiny.

I discovered that she never thought more than three days ahead. How she felt at the moment was a combination of how she had been treated in the last three days and what plans she had brewing for the weekend. I don't think she ever thought about what she might or could be doing five years down the road.

What was the point? What was going to happen was going to happen, and there wasn't much she could do but ride it out. In her mind, everything that happened in her life, good and bad, was outside her control. The upside to that mentality is that no control means no responsibility, and, of course, no responsibility means no guilt. Don't worry, she seemed to feel. Be happy. Ultimately, she had abdicated control over her life and was incapable of acting strategically in her own best interest.

It's the same with communities. The extent to which a community deals with the demographic and economic challenges ahead may depend on how well their leaders apply this gumption cycle in their civic deliberations.

It still mystifies me how a room full of community leaders who have applied the gumption cycle to their own lives and organizations with great skill and confidence cannot seem to transfer it to their community.

It's the same process. It may be harder to apply at the community level because there are a lot more people and interest groups to convince. But that's what leadership is. Leaders that believe that their community's economy and demographics are outside their field of influence are going to be incapable of acting strategically. Communities led by people who believe they have influence over their community's future are going to be the winners. Those that don't believe have abdicated their responsibility over the future. Now more than ever, it's important to know if your leaders believe, think, care, plan and have the will to invest.

Discretionary Resource Rule

This is probably a good place to talk about the Discretionary Resource rule. Most of our time and resources are already committed when we get up Monday morning. Only a small percentage of our time and resources are actually discretionary in the sense that we can choose how to spend them. Organizations and communities are the same way. Whether the ratio of time and resources already committed to those over which you have total discretion is 90/10 or 80/20, it's the only real asset you have to invest in changing what will otherwise be. In some ways, it's the most important asset you own.

Given the precious nature of discretionary time and resources, great care should be taken to invest them where they will do the most good. Spreading your discretionary time and resources around too many priorities is a prescription for failure.

These principles may seem obvious when laid out like this. Still, think about how many individuals, organizations and communities don't choose the right things to work on, or spread their time and money over too many priorities. How a community invests its discretionary time and resources will tell you a lot about its character and its chances to shape the future.

Political Factions

Undoubtedly, the biggest problem facing most communities is the conflict between internal, market-share factions and political factions that form to wield power and influence. Every town has a mix of local political factions, and between them they make most of the community's decisions. Towns with populations between 10,000 and 60,000 will have five or six factions, while metro areas have more and are harder to map. But understanding the factions and the dynamics between them are going to be central to any effort to lead or manage a community's future.

Factions form for different reasons. They form around tension points in the community. They develop as opposing or competing interests aligned against each other. Old timers may be worried about newcomers taking over. Ethnic, racial and religious differences are more common than most communities want to admit. And it is going to get worse as our communities become more diverse. Lines have long been set between the haves and have-nots, and that is likely to worsen too. Pro-growth vs. no-growth, right vs. left, agricultural heritage vs. urbanization, historical preservation vs. new development. The list is long. You'll want to understand how these tensions are driving the agendas of your ruling factions.

Finding leaders who are willing to go into the messy business of acquiring political power and wielding it in pursuit of the community's overarching interests is getting harder to do. It used to be an honor to be put up for election to public office by your fellow citizens. Now you have to wonder why any sane person with a life would voluntarily subject themselves and their families to what is essentially a never ending public trial. You can kiss off getting anything done in places with vicious local politics, where a revolving door of bitter factional rivals take turns paying each other back.

In many places, politics has become a mean, money-driven game of political gotcha. Some big cities seem to be dealing with this coarsening of politics more than smaller communities. When it happens in smaller jurisdictions, it's difficult to recover from. The fact is that leadership is going to play an even bigger role in communities that are on the bubble.

When historians look back on the last half of the twentieth century, they are going to spend a lot of time trying to figure out why we allowed the destruction of the three most important professions to modern democracy: teaching, news reporting and politics. In this era of increasing demographic diversity and economic imbalance, having the ability to develop competent leaders who can manage the factions is going to be another differentiator.

The Tips Club Factor

The issues at work creating factions seem to be getting more numerous and contentious. The crux of the leadership character issue is this: How well is the community managing these tensions and balancing the interests of the factions against the broader interests of the community? One of the biggest differentiators is the extent to which the leaders of the factions managing the community see themselves in the same boat, and the extent to which they can convince their constituents to subordinate their interests to the rest of the community.

For example, it's a constant struggle for the leaders of local economic development organizations to keep their members focused on growing the community's economy—the market—and discouraging them from using their participation to advance their share of the market. If the main reason your members are participating in civic affairs is to increase their market share, you are going to have trouble getting anything done.

This is why in a community like Omaha, Nebraska, where the majority of the leadership players represent national or global interests with no local competitors, it's easier for them to stay focused on the community. Their relationships with the others are not complicated by local turf and market-share issues.

When most of the players are competing against each other for local market share to stay alive or grow, it's a lot tougher to get consensus on a plan and stay the course. In some areas, it seems that the main reason anyone joins the leadership ranks is to gain advantage over local market-share competitors. Leadership groups dominated by these people are really just tips clubs masquerading as community benefactors.

It's hard to keep things moving in the right direction when the guy you just spent two hours with trying to figure out how to make the community better is out in the hall on his cell phone with a city councilor trying to screw you over. You want to be careful with players with dominant market-share motives.

They morph into Goat Killers and program saboteurs overnight. Thus the Tips Club Factor is another big differentiator to look for. It's going to be more prevalent as the zero-sum game sets in.

Rank Your Economic Development Effort

One way to know whether a community has its leadership act together is to look at its economic development efforts. There are basically five levels, ranging from hostile to strategic elite.

Hostile

A community gets ranked hostile when its leaders make deliberate moves to run off its economic base. Leaders in a hostile community do not understand how their economy works. They believe that growth of the economic base is the cause of unwanted population growth and sprawl, damages the environment and causes overcrowding of schools and the traffic grid. A hostile leadership group often has a strong sense of economic self-determination, but uses their confidence and skill to destroy the economic base instead of growing it. They know there is an economic development game, but they see it as an immoral form of corporate welfare that diverts critical resources away from more important priorities.

Politics in a hostile community is usually made up of environmental or social issues champions who believe that most business people are driven by greed and bent on the social and economic exploitation of a community's families and tax-dependent institutions. They believe that most of the community's problems are caused by business. They often mistakenly assume that their local businesses are dependent on the community, instead of it being the other way around.

Hostiles presume that companies that have been operating in the community for a while cannot move without going out of business, and thus are essentially hostages. In addition to being suspicious, condescending and hostile to prospective new employers, leaders openly promote punitive regulatory and tax proposals. If there is still an organized economic development effort in a town like this, it is in hiding.

Hostile leadership groups have a hard time staying in power for more than one election cycle in this day and age because the economy is so volatile. Their terms don't usually go on past the first plant closing or major downturn in tax revenue, but they can set a community back decades. In a very short period of time, great and permanent damage can be done to the economic base, the business climate and the community's reputation as a stable place in which to invest. In the past, when the community finally came to its senses and elected a more responsible city council, it had time to recover. In this new labor-constrained era, even a short period of such hostility could be fatal.

Clueless and Apathetic

The next level up from Hostile is Clueless and Apathetic. At this level, the community's leaders don't believe they have any influence over the future of their economy, or they are so demoralized they don't care anymore. They think that since many jobs are lost from forces outside the community's control, new jobs must mysteriously materialize in the same way. Jobs and opportunities just happen. No planning or effort on the community's part is needed, or even expected, to make it happen. They cannot imagine any benefit to doing anything beyond maintaining the community's infrastructure, catching criminals and keeping the town clean.

The city manager might get interested in a project if it were brought to him on a silver platter, but there are no plans, no preparation, no marketing and no efforts to create new capacity to even take advantage of an opportunity if it came along. If they know that there is an economic development game, they don't even pretend to play. They are usually waiting for the state or federal government to bring them economic development. They track no data about their economy or population; they have no economic development organization, no plan, no budget, no capacity and probably no activity.

Oddly, many of the Clueless and Apathetic class communities are irrationally selective. They can't tell you a single example of an employer or economic activity they would like to see in the future, but can articulate a long list of things they don't want, and why. Clueless communities are usually losing ground and don't even know it.

Tooth Fairy

The Tooth Fairy level can also be called the Delusional or Faking It level. At this level the community's leaders talk a great game, but are actually doing nothing. They got elected by saying they were going to do economic development, they have an economic development organization, and they fund economic development positions so they can take credit for anything good that happens and say they are supporting it even though they aren't. They really don't believe they have any influence on what is happening to them. No one has any idea about how to measure the return on the community's investment in economic development, and the leaders have mastered the art of obfuscation. Look past the rhetoric and organizational veneer and you'll see that there are no goals, no strategy, no plan, no metrics and no real investment.

The people hired to do it are faking it. There is no accountability, and of course, no results. The time, money and effort invested by public and private interests go down a rathole. Ultimately, the community's leaders have created expectations that they will do something to grow the local economy, but they have no idea how it works or what to do. Maybe they can't agree on what to do, or they don't want to risk failing. Basically, they have decided to put the community's economic development budget under the pillow and wait for the Tooth Fairy.

Sometimes community leaders are bamboozled by the professional economic development staff into thinking there's a plan and that it's being executed when it is not. Community leaders who do not understand how their local economy works are unlikely to demand to see a plan with hard number performance metrics and a return on investment calculation before investing. Tooth Fairy level programs are most common when the public sector is providing a majority of the funding. They become less common when the private sector is running the program.

Another way that local leaders are able to maintain the masquerade of economic development is to have multiple economic development organizations all professing to do economic development. With all these organizations out there, no one can say for sure that they aren't doing anything. As economic development got harder and more complicated over the years, more and more communities started faking it. It's getting harder to do now as local public and private institution budgets tighten and funding becomes more difficult. Economic development efforts are going to have to demonstrate to both their public and private sector sponsors that they are earning a tangible return on investment.

Tactical Opportunistic

Communities at the Tactical Opportunistic level are usually pretty competent at jumping on opportunities even though they may lack the vision, the plan, the unity and the discipline to truly design and develop a new economy by volition. Most of the communities that are doing a competent job at economic development year in and year out are at this level.

They know what an economic base job is, and that it's good for the community, but they are not using the E > P equation to measure for effectiveness. As a result, they are not thinking strategically.

They know what to do when presented with an economic development opportunity. They respond professionally and are investing in initiatives to fill gaps in their capacity to attract, grow and start up employers. They are likely to have a well organized, private-sector-led economic development organization staffed by skilled professionals. The community's business and public-sector organizations come together in an efficient and coordinated way when presented with a viable job creation opportunity. They know how to get things done, but they are doers, not planners. Their operational time horizon is less than three years, and they operate on a project-by-project basis.

Communities at the Tactical Opportunistic level are, for the most part, reacting to opportunities and applying their resources on a tactical level. They are performing. They often rationalize that since they don't control enough factors of production to make it worth investing resources in the "vision thing," it's too risky.

Political opponents will point to any shortfall in stated expectations as failure, and charge them with incompetence. They rationalize away return on investment standards for economic development programs as too hard and too expensive to develop and enforce.

Tactical communities have leaders that can distinguish between economic base jobs and service jobs, and may have their economic base targets picked out. They probably can't tell you what five or six major economic sectors make up the community's economic base, their relative proportions, the average wages or what incremental changes have taken place in each sector over the last five or ten years. They can't tell you what they want it to look like ten years from now, either. They may have a general idea, but their goal is abstract in that there is no quantitative definition to their expectations.

Community leaders at this level generally know what the community's problems are, but don't measure them in a way that helps them to prioritize or manage them. They have no idea what is happening on the population side of the equation, and usually don't want to know. Spending time and money finding out that your school system is failing, or that you can't attract and hold onto talent, won't help you win the next deal.

In fact, having that kind of information on the internet might hurt marketing efforts and kill future deals.

At the Opportunistic Level, community and institution leaders representing local education, health, and environmental interests will support a job-creation project, or at the very least, not fight it. But there is no common planning forum where all these other interests are regularly convened to consider how to chart the community's economic and demographic future. Political factions "live and let live," but they don't cooperate beyond the scope of an individual project opportunity.

In the labor-constrained environment we are heading into, operating at this level is going to continue to work for talent-magnet communities. If communities on the bubble and those with loser profiles want to survive, they will need to elevate their game to the Strategic Elite level.

Strategic Elite

There are very few communities operating at the Strategic Elite level because it requires leadership and program continuity through a couple of decades of election and business cycles. It is rarely reached and difficult to maintain even after it has been proven successful. It takes an extraordinary corps of inspired leaders who know how the local economy works, believe they can influence the future, and have the patience and persistence to work at a long-term strategy. They know how to get things done and are willing to put the community's welfare ahead of their own market share and ideological interests.

Strategic Elite communities invest a lot of time and money getting a data-driven sense of what is going on inside and outside the community. On the economy side of the equation, they can tell you specifically what sectors of the economic base they are going to try to grow, by how many jobs, the investment required, the number of corporate locations they will need every year in each sector, the gaps in the retail service sector that they want to fill, and the goals for net worth and household income. This type of leader can cite actual numbers when they talk about economic development.

They don't just talk about the economy side of the equation. They can tell you how many people are going to live in the community in the future, what is happening to the dependency ratio, how fast the workforce is aging, how immigration and emigration is affecting the supply of qualified workers, how the schools are performing, where they think future gaps in the supply of qualified labor are going to occur, and which initiatives are or are not working. Most importantly, a wide cross-section of leaders can give a vivid description of what the community will look and feel like ten and twenty years from now.

The community's leaders are using a common, mental construct, E >P, economy growing faster than the population, and the same nomenclature for their deliberations. They measure everything, and thus have a data-driven sense of reality. They have a specific future designed, a plan to get there, and the management skills, resources and the power to really make it happen. They have successfully enlisted the support and collaboration of all the major political and market factions. They are practicing the art of Economic Architecture: designing their future economy by pure volition. Because of demographic realities, many communities now face the daunting challenge of figuring out how to operate at this level.

Personality Position and Performance

Leadership is the application of three types of power and influence: of personality, position, and planning and performance. Some people have the charisma, communication skills and the gravitas to get people to do things they otherwise probably wouldn't want to do. Having a personality and personnel that are strong, likeable and trustworthy is important.

Courage is going to be important too. The capacity to empathize with people with opposing values and worldviews and get them to work together is going to be crucial at the local level. But, personality only goes so far.

Eventually you have to exert influence over budgets, and that often requires position. A mayor or city councilor with the deciding vote can lead. The incoming president of your economic development organization or community college can lead by declaring organizational priorities and pushing a focused agenda. People in positions of authority can lead by wielding both the carrot and the stick. Successful political leaders become masters at threatening and rewarding at the same time. We all know a title doesn't make a leader, but it helps.

The most important and most overlooked source of power is the ability to develop achievable goals, a linear path of intermediate milestones needed to get there, and to measure and manage progress. Sometimes leadership is achieved with the sheer energy, commitment and resolve of one person knocking out the milestones on his or her own. People want to be part of a winning effort. Even more importantly, they don't want to be left out of something that looks like it is going to succeed. If you initially don't have many people following you, it's okay. More will join when you start making progress.

Persistence Patience and Love

The last thing I want to leave you with on the leadership subject is something I learned from a Japanese master potter named Manji Inoue. In a life-long quest to get to the essence of things and to determine the factors that drive spectacular success, I had been seeking out and interviewing people I thought had mastered their fields and may have discovered what elements or factors predict success.

When I was doing the economic development job in Rio Rancho in the late 1980s, a friend was teaching in the art department at the University of New Mexico. She told me about an eighty-year-old ceramic potter from Japan who came to UNM every two or three years to vacation, conduct seminars and sell a few of his pieces. Incidentally, his work went for tens of thousands of dollars.

Sensei Manji Inoue was an exalted member of Japanese society who had earned the title of National Living Treasure for his work in reviving and mastering an ancient art of ceramic pottery making. My deal with my friend in the art department was that I would treat Sensei's staff to several rounds of golf during their stay in Albuquerque if I could interview him for two hours each time he came.

He lived in a compound in Japan where he invited the most promising young potters in the world to come and develop their craft. In my first interview with him I told him I was trying to learn the secrets of success in life and wondered if he would share with me what he had learned about what human characteristics he thought predicted a future master in his craft. I told him some of the things I had learned to look for when I was scouting young swimmers for the next world record holder.

I think the question I asked was, "How do you recognize talent?" His answer surprised me, but it is instructive. He said that they didn't have a word in Japanese that translates to talent in the way I was using it. He said that there were three attributes that all future masters exhibit early in their careers: persistence, patience, and love.

We spent quite a while refining, through the interpreter, what he meant by persistence and patience. I had always considered them the same. Sensei Inoue said they were very different and rarely found in the same person.

Persistence meant that the student comes to the wheel every day with total and complete concentration, with consistency, intensity and focus. He said that often people with what Americans call talent are able to acquire skills too quickly and never develop the discipline and dedication needed to break through the plateaus one inevitably encounters on the way to mastering something.

Patience is necessary if you are to avoid being defeated by frustration. He also referred to it as wisdom and maturity, and considered it a sign that the student had risen to a higher level of commitment.

Love, he said, was probably the most important. When I asked how he could tell if a student had this attribute, he said he could tell by the way the student approached the wheel, handled the clay and how he left the wheel for a break. When a student had to leave the wheel for some reason, he could tell by the way they draped the cloth over the piece and backed away, looking at it for a second before turning their back on it to leave. These subtle, nonverbal signs of a higher level of reverence and respect for the material, tools and subject were a strong predictor of success. He could also tell a lot by how a student talked about their work.

The best communities exhibit the same attributes. Persistence is important because none of the problems I am talking about are easy or solvable in the short term. They are intractable and will take a relentless, long-term effort to turn around. Patience is required too. Don't give up when progress is slow. Don't beat yourselves up, and don't beat up others who are trying to help. These problems are complicated and have been years in the making. They aren't going to get fixed in the next election cycle. But most of all, honor, love and respect your community. It is one of the most important things in your life. Efforts to make the community better are not only good for you, your family and friends, but they're noble because they will benefit the lives of people living in the community now and in the future—people you don't even know.

When you look for the signs that a community has the right stuff, screen for local leaders and managers who demonstrate persistence, patience and love in their approach to managing the community's future.

So let's review this section:

1. Communities are important, and are going to be even more important.
2. They are complex systems and are like people.
3. The economy needs to grow faster than the population, or the community can't improve.
4. The qualified quadrant of the population needs to grow faster than the others or you are screwed.
5. Leaders must believe they have influence over the future of their communities.

Part Three

Catastrophic Full Employment

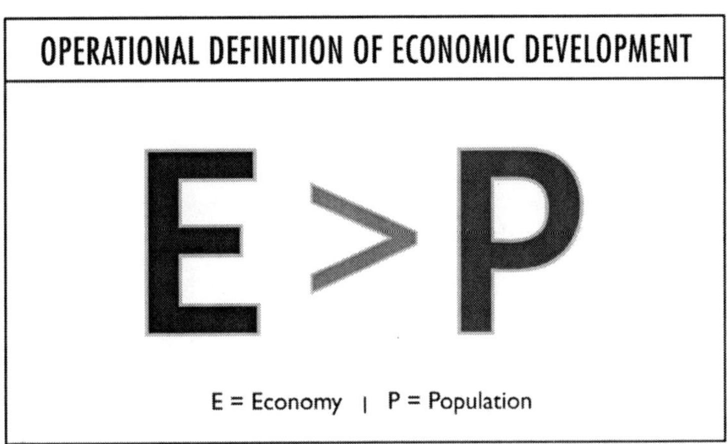

Chapter 9

Realities of a Zero-sum Labor Market

Imagine a world where your gain means someone else's ruin. In a zero-sum labor market, there won't be enough qualified workers to grow the economy faster than the population. It creates a shrinking pie where increasing market share is the only way to grow. If your company or community needs more qualified workers to grow, you will have to steal them from one of your competitors. Your growth directly diminishes one or more of your competitors. Your success now must come at someone else's expense. This is a true change in the economic development paradigm.

It is going to change the nature of the economy and the nature of the key relationships that make up civilized society. It will change the calculus of our strategic decisions, and it will soon change the way we feel about each other.

Land, Labor and Capital, plus Technology

The relationship between the three primary factors of economic production—land, labor and capital—is changing. Actually, you might say that there is a fourth factor of production in play now: technology. Until recently, land and capital were the most important variables in economic development. Labor was a minor concern because it was always in excess of demand and could migrate. Until late last century, land (natural resources and location) and capital were the hardest to come by and relatively immobile.

It used to be that if your community had coal, iron ore, barge waterways and proximity to big markets, you could develop an efficient manufacturing center, say for automobiles. Labor was relatively less important because most of the work did not require a high degree of education, and the world was awash in excess workers in need of jobs, so much so that unions were needed to keep employers from taking advantage of employees, and later, to restrict access and keep the chronic oversupply of workers from depressing wages and benefits.

As the market for automobiles grew, your community became the location for many of the industry's critical suppliers and services as well. Soon you were generating and controlling your own capital. And along with increasing commerce, capital and population came increasing political power.

Once an industry cluster approached a certain critical mass, it was virtually impossible for a competitor in another community to take it away from you. The host community's economic base was relatively secure, and its residents could expect to live long and prosper.

Today, technology makes capital and natural resources much more mobile. Mass customization, creative destruction and global competition are all conspiring to make defending market share, or staying in business, much harder. It also makes your community's economic base more tentative and volatile than ever.

A zero-sum labor market elevates qualified labor to the most important swing variable in the economic development equation. Now, creating qualified workers is more important than creating new jobs, and it's harder to do than boosting demand and production.

The population side of the E > P equation is now the weak side. There are going to be lots of jobs, but not enough qualified workers. This sudden reversal is going to create havoc *and* opportunity.

Until now, investment rules have favored hard assets, capital formation and consumption over education and training. Smart companies, communities and countries will have to figure out how to change investment rules and provide incentives for education and training in the areas the future economies will need.

Virtue to Avarice

The chronic glut of qualified labor was the basis for the enlightened logic that we could afford to be fair and generous in our relationships with each other. At the heart of the philosophy of capitalism is the theoretical presumption that everyone and anyone can improve without hurting someone else. When the pie is expanding faster than the population, your prosperity and achievement is more likely to be viewed by others as a virtuous act of initiative and mutual benefit.

Individual success in an expanding market is relatively free of negative consequences for others. You don't have to feel guilty when you win. More importantly, others don't have to feel victimized. In fact, in an expanding market you can actually lose market share and still end up with more than you had before.

But when the pie is shrinking, it's a different world. Even more market share doesn't guarantee you'll be better off. A bigger piece of the pie for you means a smaller piece for someone else, usually the weak and less able. Your success is more likely to be viewed as excessive and unfair. Your continued success will look more like predatory greed than the just rewards of virtue, good planning and hard work.

This zero-sum labor market we are heading into is going to change the fundamentals of many of the key relationships in society. In addition to influencing how we view each other, it is going to affect the motivations for joining interest groups, associations and political parties. It is going to cause groups and associations to question their missions and alliances. It will change the power relationship between employers, workers, suppliers and industry competitors.

There are especially big changes in store for the relationship between educational institutions and their clients—parents, students, workers and employers. Local leaders are going to view neighboring communities much differently when they realize that the loss of their home-grown talent impoverishes their community and enriches their rivals. It is going to affect the way competing states, nations and trading blocs view each other in the future, too. It's difficult to think of a part of our economy or society that is not going to be rocked by the realities of a zero-sum labor market.

A New Definition of Patriotism

As I said earlier, it used to be that if the kids across the street dropped out of school because their parents failed to get them to school and ready to learn, it was, well, too bad. It was sad from a humanitarian standpoint, but it meant less competition for your kids. It didn't hurt anyone but them, and it wasn't going to doom the community or the country.

In the future, that family's neglect of their children's education will be viewed more harshly. Some may even consider it tantamount to economic treason. While not as violent or as overt as joining Al Qaeda, it may be just as subversive.

As it dawns on people that having more kids and getting them educated is critical to the survival of the Republic, it could change our definition of patriotism. I expect to see new honor bestowed on those brave and able enough to have a third or fourth kid and get them through college.

If you are unable or unwilling to serve your country by having a couple of extra kids, and get them through college, then you can do your part by working with and helping neighborhood kids and young adults get an education. Some may consider it the patriotic equivalent of military service for those too old, unable or unwilling to serve.

We are bound to see a slew of incentives by national governments to encourage people to have more kids and get them educated. As I noted earlier, the Japanese are giving $80,000 to parents on the birth of their fourth child. The Russian government has procreation holidays where everyone of child-bearing age gets to go home and have sex. Look for the U.S. government to start offering tax incentives and giving preferential treatment to parents who have three or more kids and who get them through school.

The damage done by parents who neglect their social responsibility to get themselves and their kids educated is going to become more obvious. Attitudes are going to change. In addition to new incentives, I expect a movement to overhaul truancy laws and the development of other punitive measures to coerce negligent parents and their kids to focus on their responsibilities. But it won't be a one-way discussion.

There's already a large underclass of dependents and those unprepared to learn or earn. As they watch their numbers grow and their chances for prosperity shrink, they will continue to see themselves as victims. Both sides will be right. Civil debate over who is to blame and what carrots and sticks should be used to turn things around will probably get ugly.

Power to the People

One of the most significant changes now underway is the power shift in the hiring relationship between employers and workers. It will take a while to sink in and sort out, but as we shift from a structural oversupply of qualified labor to a structural shortage, the power over who gets a job is shifting from the employer to the worker.

In 1971 when I graduated from college and started looking for a job, I was part of the greatest flood of qualified workers ever to hit the planet. In the 1960s and 1970s in the U.S.

alone, more than 78 million Boomers got out of school and headed into the workforce. It was brutal. Every time there was a decent job opening there were ten of us in the lobby filling out applications, hoping to get the job.

When they finally offered one of us the job, the conversation went something like, "Okay Mr. Lautman, we have decided to offer you the job. Congratulations. However, it's only half the salary you were asking for, and you'll have to move to Cleveland on your own dime."

When that happened we thought we had hit the jackpot. It was the only way to get a career going. We were grateful. The employer had all the power.

In the future, when a decent job comes up for grabs, there may only be one qualified candidate, and there will be ten companies in hot pursuit. The shoe will be on the other foot. The candidate will be interviewing the employer. The candidates will be saying, "You know, I really like you and your firm. I like your mission and values. You are leading the green movement in your industry. I would get to work with some of the smartest people in my career field and on really interesting projects. I especially like the flexible work rules and the chances for advancement. But you know, I always wanted to live somewhere where I could ski on my days off. If you can get me a condo at the base of Al's Run at Taos Ski Valley, and a little bigger signing bonus, I'll think about giving you two years."

People with education, skills, experience and work ethic will be in a position to extort compensation and work rules from employers that Boomers never dreamed of. Power to the people!

The Rise of the Human Resources Manager

Human resource managers all over the world are scrambling to figure new ways to find talent and make them more productive so they can afford to pay them enough to hang onto them. For three years, I was part of a national think tank called the Design Collaborative on the Future of Work. A couple of retired Berkeley professors, Jim Ware and Charlie Grantham, convened a group of human resources, information technology and senior managers from twenty-three of the country's largest technology-dependent employers to explore the frontiers of the future of work.

This is where I was first exposed to the lengths talent-dependent companies were prepared to go to in order to deal with what they saw as the imminent interruption in their workforce pipeline of talent. Most of the companies represented were in the Fortune 500, and each was a leader in their respective industry.

The group was put together so there were no direct competitors involved. Everyone signed non-disclosure agreements to prevent proprietary data and strategies from being leaked.

Most of the think tank participants were the people heading up research efforts within their respective companies. Most of the research was focused on how to restructure their organizations, work processes, work rules and management practices to make them more attractive to the incoming generations of workers.

One of the toughest issues was how to reconcile the wildly contrasting preferences and work styles of the Boomer, Gen X, Gen Y and the Millennial generations.

Three times a year Jim and Charlie conducted a two-and-a-half-day charrette—a fancy French word that architects now use instead of "meeting."

At each session, each member of the Collaborative would present a twenty-five-minute summary of the challenges they were facing, the research they were doing and the conclusions they were drawing. An equal amount of time was budgeted for the group to critique and share ideas.

It was there that I began to learn of the efforts companies were making to understand what made these temperamental, new, tech-savvy workers tick.

It was clear in 2003 that Jim's and Charlie's companies understood that they would not survive if they could not prevail in the world labor market. They were prepared to do whatever it took. Everything was on the table—more flexible work rules, more training and orientation, mentoring training for managers, self-directed team project management models, sabbaticals, continuing-education strategies, preventive health programs and more.

When the Design Collaborative group began to wind down going into the recession, many of the companies had already retooled their site-selection strategies to find locations where talent was headed.

One participant reported that she learned that one of her competitors was planning to start signing standout high school chemistry students in their sophomore and junior years. If the Yankees can go after a kid with an eighty-mile-an-hour fastball in his junior year, why can't we go after his classmate who understands thermodynamics at age sixteen? Who knows, someday we may see a professional draft for science and technical students.

As the realities of a zero-sum labor market set in, personnel managers will no longer focus on merely grading resumes, administering benefits packages and updating the employee handbook. Today, human resource managers are the point-of-the-spear for corporate strategic planning and site selection. Look for the same thing to happen soon in the public sector.

Public-Sector versus Private-Sector Employers

The tables may turn on public-sector employers, as well. In this new environment they could find it more difficult to meet critical staffing levels than their private-sector counterparts. Many public employees have better health insurance and retirement packages than their private-sector counterparts, which tempt them to retire earlier. That is creating critical vacancies in government agencies.

But the real risk to public-sector employers in this environment is that they could lose their primary competitive edge in the market, which is job security. Back in the day, careers in government were popular because there were not enough jobs in the private sector to go around. The risk of losing a private-sector job to a more productive worker, offshore competition or the business cycle was enough to convince the most risk-averse workers to trade the prospect of higher wages, more interesting work and potential for faster advancement for the job security of the public sector.

But government jobs aren't as safe as they used to be. And they will be harder to protect as government institutions at every level have to serve more people with less revenue. We may even see a regulatory movement that puts public-sector institutions under the same return-on-investment scrutiny that the private sector has had to deal with. Now the tradeoff doesn't look so good. Look for government employers to begin elevating their human resource game. They are going to have to come up with something besides job security if they expect to attract and hold qualified workers in a zero-sum labor market.

The End of Discrimination in the Workplace?

Another aspect of the employer/employee relationship that promises to see a dramatic change is the problem of workplace discrimination. In the past, an employer that allowed hiring and promotions to be based on personal preferences or prejudices towards candidates of a particular racial, ethnic, gender, lifestyle, religious or political group might be able to survive. In the future, employers competing for a shrinking pie of qualified workers won't be able to afford bigotry.

The zero-sum labor market is going to do more to end discrimination in the workplace than the Equal Employment Opportunity Commission and Affirmative Action ever did. In a labor-starved market, employers won't care about your ethnicity, race, gender, age, or anything else except your ability to do the job.

If you are qualified to do the work, the other stuff won't matter. If you are the only applicant, you'll get hired. And if you are any good, they'll be bending over backwards to keep you. If there is discrimination, it will be in the other direction. Workers will discriminate against employers if they don't feel comfortable with their values.

This is not to say that workplace discrimination will end. When I spoke at an NAACP-LULAC regional conference a few years ago, I made the mistake of showing them the Inverted Labor Supply Curve and suggesting that their organizations should at least consider the possibility that, in the future, their biggest problem might not be employer bigotry.

If I had taken a little more time to get to know my audience I might have been able to make these points a little more diplomatically. I got some pretty nasty heckling from the crowd. What really got people riled up was my suggestion that they think about shifting some of their resources from suing employers to suing the school systems that are dropping their kids in the dirt.

I tried to explain that the Inverted Labor Supply Curve might solve a big part of the problem. In a zero-sum labor market, no employer needing qualified workers will be able to discriminate on any factor except education and the ability to do the work. Discrimination on the basis of ethnic or racial prejudices will be solved by demographics. I told them that focusing their resources on suing bigoted employers was likely to yield diminishing returns. The market is going to put them out of business before they can.

I said that in the next twenty-five years it would be the incompetence and negligence of the people running their kids' school districts that would screw their constituents over. I also made a comment about the heavy lifting their leadership and the education profession would have to do to simultaneously raise standards, get kids to take harder classes and keep them in school. That didn't go down well either.

The reality is that the power shift from employer to worker is only going to affect jobs that require education and skill. There simply will be no shortage of uneducated and unskilled workers.

In fact, unqualified workers are heading into a terrible market that only promises to get worse. If you don't get an education and learn some skills, you are going to be in a situation where you have tons of new competitors enter your market every day who will be willing to work for a lot less than you can live on.

In a zero-sum labor market, anyone unable or unwilling to acquire the education, skills and experience to qualify for the jobs in demand will continue to need legal protection from unfair hiring and promotion practices.

Chickens Coming Home to Roost

The upshot of all this is that education now trumps ethnicity, lifestyle, gender and everything else. Discrimination will be based on educational achievement and experience, not race or gender. Get an education and some training and you'll get a good job. Don't, and you'll stay in the underclass.

As talent becomes scarcer, the value of education and training will rise. Everyone who pays for educational services is going to demand better quality and more choices. At some point, community leaders, employers, parents and workers will begin to realize that we have been sold down the river by the education profession and their lobby who have basically rigged the system to protect their jobs at the expense of their students, their communities and their country.

Public schools and universities are going to be hit hard on two levels by the Boomer retire-off and the shortage of qualified workers—maybe harder than the private sector. They are going to lose a disproportional number of teachers to retirement, and they are going to take a lot of political heat for the shortage of qualified workers.

In a zero-sum labor market, qualified teachers won't need unions for job security. Eventually, the leaders of our minority populations and social justice advocates will snap to the fact that their friends running the education system are the ones holding them back, not the employers.

Higher education institutions are going to have to make some big changes too. Like most private-sector firms, they will have to scramble to replace a rapidly retiring Boomer workforce. They will have to continue shifting precious resources to remedial education programs to finish the job that public schools are supposed to do. Simultaneously, they are going to have to realign and elevate their programs to stay in business.

I predict that program and curriculum alignment will become a big issue as we work our way into a zero-sum market. When we were raising and educating more kids than the economy could absorb every year, it didn't really matter how many graduates we produced in any discipline. Graduating hundreds of anthropologists every year when the economy only needed two didn't really hurt the local economy or the country.

If there was going to be an oversupply of qualified workers in every category anyway, then students and public educational institutions didn't have to worry about aligning and scaling their programs to the economy. Educators didn't have to be strategic about the mix and size of their academic programs.

In a zero-sum labor market, we will need to be strategic about our investment in educational institutions. A community's interests and the interests of the university may not be served by continuing to invest in producing ten times the number anthropologists than it looks like the economy is going to need as critical shortages develop for nursing and engineering graduates.

Everyone knows we have a big problem. Eventually, the education profession will realize that they have to discipline their own ranks and support the draconian measures now required to fix the system. If we don't dramatically reduce the dropout rate and realign the system to produce the qualified workers needed for critical career paths, we will starve the economy of the workers we need to produce the tax revenue needed to fund their salaries.

Maybe the only profession more at risk from a zero-sum labor market is the economic development profession. If we don't get our act together soon we will end up on the endangered species list along with travel agents and elevator operators.

Stress on the Economic Development Relationship

One of the purposes of this chapter is to get you to think about how a zero-sum labor market will change the relationship between economic base employers and their host communities. I call this the Economic Development Relationship. Economic development programs at the state and local levels have primarily focused on managing the relationship between economic base employers and the community.

At the foundation of the relationship is a covenant. On one side, economic base employers bring all the new money in, providing the reason for the community to exist.

On the other side, the community provides the ecosystem that the economic base employers need to thrive against their global competitors. By ecosystem, I mean things like location, amenities, infrastructure, workforce, capital, business climate and an economic base employers need today to survive. It's a co-dependent relationship if there ever was one. And like most co-dependent relationships, both sides think they are holding the short end of the stick.

The Site-Selection Process

The site-selection process usually starts when a company begins to run out of capacity. Someone in the organization begins thinking about where and how they should expand. Occasionally, the process is triggered by a conclusion that they have to move the operations out of a hostile or uncompetitive location. Other reasons that might make an employer footloose include an impending sale, merger or downsizing of the company.

In any case, management usually forms a secret committee representing some or all of the company's critical departments or divisions. Secrecy is crucial to prevent speculation by key employees, suppliers and competitors.

The committee goes through the company's operating costs and weighs the factors that they believe will allow them to lower costs, reduce risk and gain advantage over competitors. Sometimes, in small companies, this process is conducted entirely by the owner.

Over the years, as competition increased and employers became more sophisticated about managing their variable costs, the job of developing this criteria and the process for selecting a new site has become much more complicated and scientific.

In the old days, the CEO or owner would call an industrial real estate broker or a site-selection consultant and have them scour the country for communities with high unemployment and empty buildings.

Now it's different. A company's site-selection committee, with the help of its site-selection consultant, now develops a decision matrix. Down the left side of the matrix will be a list of twelve to two hundred operational cost line items or variables that drive the firm's profitability. Across the top they list all the communities or sites under consideration.

With cost data from each community logged into a spreadsheet, it's relatively easy to determine which communities are most competitive.

By this time they have a pretty good idea how their balance sheet will look if they operate in any of the communities under consideration. At this point, they go back to the highest ranked communities and pit them against each other to see which one will give them the best deal.

The number of factors on the decision matrix and their relative weight in the decision will vary wildly depending on the industry and the individual firm. This makes it dangerous to generalize about what employers want in a location, and conversely, what makes one community more attractive than another. But I'm going to generalize anyway.

For the sake of analysis, I would divide the types of economic base enterprises into three general categories: logistics-driven, tax-and-regulatory-driven and labor-driven. Not coincidentally, the site-selection consultants have specialized and organized their practices in the same way.

Logistics-driven enterprises like warehousing, freight forwarding and distribution centers tend to have only two variable costs—transportation and rent. So, the site-selection process will focus on finding the building with lowest rent and operating costs at the best place on the map for access to inbound and outbound traffic. Access or proximity to water, air and rail facilities is often a major consideration. But labor is not usually a big deal. They only need a few forklift drivers.

Tax and regulatory issues occasionally factor into the decision, but for the most part, it's a straight up real estate deal. As a result, most of the consultancies that do most of the site-selection work for logistics operations are housed in the big national real estate firms. They might have a tax and incentives specialist, and a demographer on staff or associated with them, but most of the staff are real estate focused.

Manufacturers often have the longest and most diverse list of variable costs to run down. They are more likely to be focused on tax and regulatory issues and need a bigger and broader team of experts to help them than do logistic and service enterprises. There are generally more state and local incentive programs for manufacturers, so their site-selection teams are likely to be led by experts in negotiating public incentives.

Economic base employers that primarily hire people to work in offices are going to be more likely to view labor as their primary variable cost.

A location-neutral business such as a call center can go virtually anywhere there is qualified labor. Many labor-driven projects can locate in a vacant store or anywhere they can get good telecommunications services.

The critical variable is labor. Their decision formula will be heavy with questions about a community's demographics. They are going to want to know how many people are in the local market with the education and skills they need.

They will try to zero in on what the wage and benefits package they will need to become the employer of choice in that market.

They will be interested in incentives, utilities, facilities and all that other stuff, but human resource considerations are usually driving the decision, and the consultants are usually heavy with labor-market analysts and demographers.

Until the late 1980s, it was rare to be grilled by a site-selection team about the local labor market. They might ask about Right to Work and the level of unionization, sometimes, but back then they always figured that qualified workers would migrate in for jobs if it turned out the local market got tight. Since then, the labor questions during the site-selection process have gotten tougher and tougher.

I'm still surprised that even now there is little useful, real-time data about local labor markets. And there's virtually no trend data.

We have already talked about how employers are rethinking their expectations and modifying their work rules to prepare for the War for Talent. The changes to the site-selection process promise to be even more dramatic on the community side of the relationship.

Just as employers have had to hire site-selection consultants, communities have had to hire economic developers to help manage the site-selection process.

The Rise of Economic Development

The economic development profession actually started in Tupelo, Mississippi, in the 1930s. The local cotton industry was failing, and the town fathers sent a couple of local guys up to Chicago to see if they could talk one of the factory owners into moving to their community. They promised to make it worth the owner's while, with free buildings, financing, low taxes and other incentives. Economic development as we practice it today was born. By the mid-1960s, every town in the country with more than 10,000 people had an economic development program. Sometimes it was one person designated to help corporate site-selection teams get the information they needed for their analysis, and to be their liaison if they wound up coming. In other places, it evolved into a major civic enterprise, complete with its own board of directors and a full-time professional staff.

The country was awash with unemployed or underemployed talent, and most community leaders didn't think there was anything wrong with their towns that a few new economic base jobs wouldn't fix. So they would raise some money, design a brochure and hire a hot-shot economic developer to get out there and find them a deal.

The Location Decision Power Shift

A zero-sum labor market substantially changes the fundamentals of the corporate site-selection process for both communities and employers. The shift of power from employer to the employee in the hiring relationship means a shift of power over where new economic base jobs will be created. Location decisions used to be made between a company's CEO and a community's mayor. The decision was subject to much more discretion from both sides than it is now.

As we move to a zero-sum labor market, CEOs and mayors will lose much of their ability to manage the site-selection process with incentives. It's going to change the nature and intensity of their relationships. They are going to be much more dependent on each other and will have to cooperate on a strategic level to create an environment capable of attracting and holding talent.

The crux of the zero-sum labor market is that for communities to grow their economies faster than their populations, it is going to come down to their ability to convince economic base employers that they are the best place in the world to ride out the war for talent.

A screaming deal on a facility, the lowest taxes, utility costs and a big incentive package will be worthless if you can't demonstrate that the community has enough qualified labor to staff the facility, is growing enough local talent, and is able to steal talent from competitors in other communities and keep them from being stolen back.

If you can't make the labor case, the new jobs aren't going to be created. The site-selection decision is completely out of the CEO and the mayor's hands—no labor, no power, no discretion, no deal, no relationship. In other words, no economic development.

The Death of Economic Development

Why do we need economic development programs? Why will city officials or local business owners write big checks every year to sponsor the local economic development organization to send someone out looking for more economic base employers when those very sponsors are failing because they can't find qualified workers? The answer is they won't.

On the other side, why would a site-selection consultant even suggest putting a community on the list to look at if there is no qualified labor available? They won't.

The economic development profession is reacting to this situation in much the same way as the education profession. They resist attempts to measure what they do. Their own organizations have been politicized, and many economic development professionals have defaulted into being bureaucrats.

Education is the only profession where the ratio of talk to action is worse than in economic development. It's really easy to talk about what's wrong and what needs to be done to fix the public school system and the local economy, but it's quite another matter getting anything done. Both professions are in for a brutal next decade as their roles, responsibilities and relationships come under more pressure and scrutiny.

Over half the communities in the country are out of the economic development game already and don't even know it. Many more will be when they hit full employment of their qualified workers. We are about to become a nation with two kinds of communities: winners and losers. Communities that are growing and attracting and holding onto more talent than leaves every year will be able to stay in the game. The others will be SOL.

Once a community starts losing talent, it will face the grim likelihood that it will enter an economic death spiral from which it will never recover.

Chapter 10

Loserville

So remember the movie *It's a Wonderful Life?* Jimmy Stewart's character, George Bailey, lives in idyllic Bedford Falls where his family is beloved for their efforts to help friends and neighbors build their own homes and businesses.

George is distraught over the imminent insolvency of Bailey Building and Loan and the prospect of Bedford Falls being taken over by the evil Mr. Potter.

Believing his life insurance makes him worth more dead than alive to his friends and family, he is about to jump off a bridge. An angel, Clarence, is sent to save him. When George declares that he wished he'd never been born, Clarence takes George on a tour of the town as it would have been had he not been born.

In the parallel world with no George Bailey, the town is a very different place. Instead of Bedford Falls, it's named Potterville. The once happy, thriving place full of warm and outgoing friends has been transformed into a seedy, mean-spirited place controlled by the evil Mr. Potter.

In Potterville, George's friends and family are ruined and despondent. Everyone in town seems to be trapped in miserable and hopeless lives.

In the story, George had put off his ambitions to finally get out of Bedford Falls and go to college and see the world.

He had been trapped into staying to keep the family business going so his younger brother could go to college and play football. The problem we'll be facing the next twenty-five years is that too many George Baileys have not been born. And the ones who have will be anxious to move to more exciting and productive places.

This is going to turn a lot of places like Bedford Falls into Pottervilles before it's over. How will it happen? Is your community a candidate? These questions are the focus of this chapter.

The coming zero-sum labor market means that as communities struggle to grow their economies faster than their populations, qualified workers will have to be lured away from other communities. Since workers will have the upper hand in the hiring relationship, they will decide where many of the new jobs go. Communities where workers want to live will gain, and those they wish to leave will lose.

We are entering a new world, one where every community will end up either a winner or a loser. This is going to be difficult enough for a society bent on fairness at all costs. But what makes it especially disconcerting is the demographic and economic situations in both the winning and losing communities. Winners will get richer, more interesting and more attractive every year at the expense of the losers.

Unable to hold onto, or attract the qualified labor they need, losing communities will be unable to staff an economy large enough to sustain their tax-dependent institutions. Without the workers, they won't be able to generate the additional economic activity needed to keep pace with a growing dependent class of residents.

I know it sounds a little melodramatic, but not when you contemplate the toll it will take on the lives of people stuck in those Loservilles.

What is the Community Death Spiral? What causes it? And what does it look like?

Loserville—The Community Economic Death Spiral

I define a Community Death Spiral as a prolonged downturn in the community's business or development cycle—one that never cycles back up for a net gain. The local economy no longer has the means to grow faster or (shrink slower) than the population.

The Community Death Spiral is caused by two things: economic starvation and demographic starvation. Economic starvation results when a community's population is deprived of the economic base jobs and investment needed to sustain itself.

Demographic starvation occurs when a community cannot field enough qualified workers to staff its economic base.

The result is the same: an economic death spiral.

Economic Base Job Starvation

In the past we only worried about job starvation scenarios.

The cycle was often triggered by an economic event such as failure of an economic base employer, falling commodity prices, tapped out natural resources or changes in transportation and utility economics.

In job starvation scenarios, all the community had to do was to find a replacement employer. Sometimes one transaction was all it took. One CEO deciding to invest in a few new jobs and the arrow in the $E < P$ equation would be pointed the right way again: $E > P$.

In the case of a closed plant, community leaders chipped in and cranked up an industrial recruiting program. They put up a spec building if they had to, put a crew on the road to find a replacement tenant, and threw in whatever incentives were needed to close the deal.

Nobody worried about labor back then. For most places, if you didn't have enough qualified labor it was assumed that qualified workers would pour in from neighboring communities.

It was a little tougher for communities suffering through agriculture or extractive market cycles. Agricultural communities would often have to build a spec building to get into the recruiting game. Convincing manufacturers to move to mining and oilfield towns in the middle of a bust period was especially difficult. Manufacturers assumed, correctly, that their employees would head back to the higher paying mines or derricks once commodity markets cycled back. Agricultural communities could shift to different crops, but oilfield and mining towns would often have to batten down the hatches and ride it out.

In the recent past, most business cycle downturns, while painful and disruptive, were not catastrophic. Communities were usually left with all the land, labor and capital they needed to recover. But sometimes it was fatal, and some places turned into ghost towns.

Once the underlying demand for the goods and services produced by a community's economic base employers disappears, there is no longer an economic reason for the community to exist. In a few decades, everyone who can, leaves to find work elsewhere. A few stay to finish out their lives and watch Mother Nature repossess what had once been.

Labor-Starvation Scenario

Labor starvation is a much different scenario. It not only is more likely now, but it is also least likely to be recognized. Turning around an economy that's contracting because it's being starved of qualified workers requires different solutions. Thousands of individual workers, retirees and students will need to be persuaded to come or stay and learn and work. In most places that are already attracting and retaining qualified labor, it means fixing some big, hairy, intractable problems first.

As retirement and emigration slowly boil off a community's qualified workforce, a growing majority of dependents and unemployable workers is left behind. It occurs so slowly that most people don't notice it. If you are still looking through the prism of the old paradigm—not enough jobs—you can't see that it's a population-side problem until it's too late.

At first, it will feel like the beginning of another downturn in a normal business cycle. The community may see occasional signs of recovery, but its economy never seems to recover. The cycle never quite reaches a bottom. When that happens, it's not a cycle anymore. It is a spiral.

The Community Economic Death Spiral

If a community is not attractive enough to steal talent from other communities and hang on to it, then it risks slipping into a long, painful and demoralizing decline. In an inverted labor supply environment, if you lack the talent to staff your economic base, and you can't steal them from other communities, you won't recover.

We all know that business cycles are an inevitable and natural fact of life. Ironically, it might be our belief in the business cycle that blinds us to what is happening.

Communities' leaders won't see it coming. They'll be like the buggy whip manufacturers who mistook a steady decline in sales as a cyclical change they needed to merely ride out, when it was actually a structural change caused by the rise of the automobile.

Like that guy on the beach in Indonesia looking at the tsunami moving toward shore, community leaders need another level of knowledge and awareness to recognize that this situation is different.

If the Indonesian had a little more knowledge, a little of the right kind of data, and a little more time, he might have figured it out that he was looking at a different tidal paradigm, and might have been able to save himself.

Many communities will slip into a death spiral oblivious and unaware. Instead of a sudden, single and catastrophic defection of a major employer, the community dies slowly from a thousand individual defections of its most qualified workers. The most qualified workers leave the workforce. The old ones retire. The younger ones leave for greener pastures.

Let's look at the mechanics of a labor-starvation-caused spiral. It starts when your community hits full employment—full employment of its qualified workforce, that is.

Phase 1: Tight Labor & Talent Flight

We start with almost all of the qualified workers in Loserville fully employed. Loserville's workforce is heavy with workers nearing retirement, and light on new ones to replace them. The population is growing slowly, but census data confirms that as qualified workers and wealthy retirees leave, they are being replaced by unprepared new entrants from a failing local school system and poor immigrants unprepared to earn or learn. The community's 64-to-84-year-old population is growing twice as fast as the 24-to-44-year-old group. The census shows that their 24-to-44-year-old age group is growing poorer and less educated than the region and the nation.

The leaders of Loserville's city and county governments, public schools, community college and regional hospital fall into two categories: those who know things are bad and getting worse, but feel powerless to do anything about it, and those with delusions of adequacy. Many of them are just trying to hold on for another year or two until they can retire.

Phase 2: Aversion to Data

The community has been desensitized to bad news by years of reports documenting its poor economic and educational rankings. There is no appetite for more data, analysis or discussion about its problems. The last thing its leaders want to do is spend precious budget resources gathering more data to prove how badly they are doing.

Most of them learned a long time ago not to bring up problems you don't have solutions for. Annual reports by Loserville's local institutions are devoid of data or straight talk about the grim realities facing the community. There is no data being gathered on the big issues, no analysis and no discussion. Anyone raising questions in public about troubling issues is ostracized as a flame-throwing naysayer.

The community's media outlets are owned and operated by out-of-state firms and are struggling financially. The local paper has half as many pages as it did a few years ago and now publishes only three days a week.

The editorial and reporting staff is young and inexperienced, poorly paid, often ignorant of the subject matter they are reporting on and politically biased. Editors are eager to inflame and exploit the most trivial controversies while they ignore the tougher, more complex issues that matter.

Having downsized in the 1990s, most of the community's economic base employers are beginning to realize that they don't have enough talent and experience coming up for a smooth succession. Talent isn't exactly streaming into town.

In fact, local leaders admit that it's hard to imagine anyone in America waking up and saying, "Gee honey, I wonder if they have any good jobs in Loserville? I've always wanted to live there." Even long-time residents who thought they would never leave find themselves wishing they lived somewhere else. The Rotary Club is getting a little smaller and older every year. Half the meetings are taken up with new retirement announcements and reports on the health emergencies of absent members.

Loserville High is getting most of its really smart kids into college even though many of them need remedial classes their freshman year. But those kids leave town as fast as they can, never to return. Of the rest, many are stuck living at home, working menial, dead-end service jobs and getting into trouble. A few ambitious ones take classes at the community college in an effort to get the education they failed to get in high school.

The high school dropout rate has been above thirty percent for the past decade. Teen pregnancy, drug abuse and juvenile crime continue rising despite recent efforts to bring them down. Educational attainment is going up slightly, but at the expense of scholastic achievement. The majority of the schools in the district do not meet the minimum federal educational standards, and local employers report that most of Loserville High's graduates are unprepared for even the most menial work. Many can't read a ruler or take simple measurements.

But the community's leaders have no economic plan for its future. If they do, no one has told the high school and community college counselors. No one is advising students or mid-career change candidates about what jobs will be in greatest demand in the near future. The community college curriculum is largely determined by what the faculty feels like teaching that semester.

Loserville has an economic development corporation, but there are no education or workforce development leaders on its executive committee. There is no intelligence coming from the Loserville EDC to help local educators, students and mid-career students make career path decisions. And there is no strategy for investing the community's dwindling discretionary resources. The economic developer they hired to fix the economy started interviewing for his next job the day after being hired.

The EDC staff spends most of their time raising funds and politicking to keep their jobs. Operating at the Tooth Fairy level, the Loserville EDC waits patiently for the state to bring them an economic development deal. The state's economic development people try to pitch Loserville to every economic base employer they see, but even though the community's facilities and incentives are among the best in the country, they never get a visit from anyone with a real balance sheet. The viable companies and their site-selection consultants can see from census, commerce and education data that the place is incapable of supporting new economic base jobs. If the data isn't clear enough, a call to a few of the community's existing employers will confirm it.

Not surprisingly, Loserville's existing economic base employers are under duress from their inability to recruit and keep talent. Competitors in more attractive communities are stealing their best people and beginning to take market share. The companies' human resource people will tell you that they have had dozens of key positions open for months.

They get plenty of interest from qualified out-of-state candidates, but their closing rates have dropped every year for the last six years. And when they get one to sign on, only one in ten makes it to their first anniversary.

The majority of local applicants lacks the education and experience, or can't pass the drug test. Many companies are running their own remedial math and language programs for new employees.

Behind the scenes, some local service sector business owners are actually sabotaging efforts to recruit new economic base employers. "I'm going broke because I can't find qualified people. Why are we trying to recruit new employers?" they say.

Local residents are beginning to talk about a noticeable decline in the quality of service from the Burger King to their auto repair shop.

Some community leaders have suggested that local employers simply raise salaries and benefits to solve the problem. But those that do find their customers fleeing to lower cost, out-of-town competitors who have been able to hold the line on wages. Undaunted, a city councilor trying to make a name for him or herself pushes a measure to double the minimum wage.

Phase 3: Economic Base Defections

At a corporate board meeting of Loserville's biggest economic base employer, concerns about the age distribution of the plant's workforce, falling productivity, and human resource's dismal recruiting performance puts the facility at the top of their downsizing list. While no decision has been made to close it yet, plans to invest in scheduled system upgrades and new equipment are postponed indefinitely.

Positions vacated by retirements, transfers or terminations will not be filled. No more step raises will be approved, even though everyone must do more work for the same pay. The plant's contracts with local suppliers are not being renewed; that business is quietly being transferred to vendors at the company's other locations.

As word spreads, a pall of uncertainty comes over the community. Locals start to cut back on spending. Listings for homes and businesses rise. Anyone considering a major investment in the community suspends negotiations. They figure they are bound to get a better deal in a few months.

State and local political leaders blame greedy, unfeeling corporate outsiders for the plant's problems. Aspiring candidates blame incumbents and vow to create jobs, jobs and more jobs. The governor comes for a strategy meeting with plant officials and local leaders. A joint press conference is held. They announce that a job fair will be held in the following month. Lots of jobs are available, and plenty of people are looking, but the skills of those looking don't match the jobs being offered.

Phase 4: Service Sector Contraction

Unable to find good help, and detecting a drop in commercial and retail activity, Loserville's service sector businesses start reducing inventory and laying off workers. The smarter owners see the writing on the wall and sell out or retire early. Unable to attract a new doctor to buy his practice, the community's only OBGYN retires and moves to Maui.

Many of the community's family-owned service businesses that survived the arrival of Wal-Mart are looking at serious succession problems of their own. These multi-generational, family-owned businesses used to define the character of the community and provided most of its leadership.

Lacking the offspring for succession, and unable to find a buyer, many of these business owners are making plans to let the business die. Routine maintenance gets deferred. New projects and business ventures are abandoned or postponed. A few brave (or stupid) ones continue burning equity while hoping their main competitor goes out of business first. Everyone is hoping to hang on until things turn around.

But in Loserville, they never do. It isn't a nosedive like past bust or recession cycles. It's a slow, almost imperceptible retrograde that produces malaise instead of a panic. But it's a death spiral nonetheless. As local stores close, residents must go to stores in competing communities. Commercial and retail property values decline. Assessed valuation for property taxes, sales tax receipts and fees income decline as well.

Phase 5: Drop in Net Worth

As the community's most productive residents are exchanged for dependents and less productive (lower paid) residents, prices for residential homes continue to drop. The net worth of the community's citizens begins to erode. As real estate values slide, equity on the balance sheets of local residents and businesses disappears. More residents are forced to rent substandard housing or opt for mobile homes that depreciate faster than they can be paid off. Those on the edge go under. Many that were doing well are pushed to the edge. Foreclosures go up. Bankruptcies increase. Spending and investment in the community declines further. Regulators force local banks to restrict credit and move more cash to reserves to cover the increasing number of loans where the value of the collateral property doesn't cover the remaining principal.

Phase 6: Tax Base Erodes and Service Burden Increases

Fewer paychecks, less spending, stores going out of business, more leakage and falling property values cause Loserville's tax base to contract. Sales tax revenues decline, assessed valuations and tax collections drop. In most places, city and county governments, school districts and hospitals are prohibited from running deficits by state law.

With the tax base shrinking and the number of dependents and their needs growing, the service burdens of Loserville's local tax-dependent institutions outgrow its revenue a little every year. So it ends up in the terrible dilemma of having to serve more people every year with less and less money. No help comes from the state or federal government. They're broke too.

Phase 7: Discretionary Investment Halts

As local tax-dependent institutions use up their reserve funds, bond ratings fall. Discretionary investment comes to a halt. There is no money for any of the things that the schools, the city, county, council of governments, the hospital or anyone else thinks needs to be done to make the community better. The community stops improving. The community *stops thinking about improving*. Attention turns to survival. The reality of a zero-sum market starts to set in. The goat killing begins.

Phase 8: Deferred Maintenance

Soon, scheduled maintenance on critical infrastructure and systems is deferred. The axiom of "Pay me now or pay me a lot more later" goes into effect, meaning the community is digging a bigger and bigger hole for itself. Eventually, potholes and water main breaks become common occurrences. Little things like landscaping and peeling paint on government buildings make the place look depressed and neglected. Qualified workers who have a choice of where to live, keep on driving past.

Phase 9: Interruption of Services

Eventually, deferred maintenance doesn't cover the deficits. Services have to be cut. It starts with a hiring freeze. Programs and services are eliminated. Sports and recreation programs are canceled, ambulance services are curtailed, and hospital emergency rooms are shut down.

Cuts are made in after-school art, music, sports, science, math and reading programs. Senior citizen programs are curtailed. It starts with reductions at animal control and eventually gets to the police and fire departments. It ends with personnel cuts throughout local government. People take early retirement or are furloughed.

Phase 10: Higher Taxes

In the end, with revenue contracting and demand for services growing, community leaders must resort to raising taxes and fees. Loserville already has one of the highest per capita tax burdens in the region, and it has been growing the fastest. This further discourages investment.

The community's economic base employers become less competitive than their competitors. Local residents and service-sector employers can buy less. Higher property and sales taxes have regressive effects on Loserville's fastest growing demographic segments: the retired, the poor and the unskilled.

It would be one thing if increased taxes resulted in improvements needed to make the community more attractive and efficient so it could compete, but they're not. The tragedy of the death spiral is that economic decline, talent flight and deferred maintenance put the goal of breaking even further off every year.

Phase 11: Goat Killing

Leadership was never really strong in Loserville to begin with; otherwise they might have been able to make the strategic investments needed to avoid entering the death spiral. But it's too late now. The problems are so intractable, and local politics is so factionalized, that no one with any political acumen wants to run for office.

The EDC, chamber of commerce, Hispano chamber, food bank, the homeless shelter, the high school booster club and political candidates increasingly view themselves to be in a cut-throat competition for a piece of a shrinking civic pie.

Political and social fractures widen into major rifts, pitting neighbors and friends against each other in an increasingly partisan and mean-spirited environment. Goat Killers and radicals rule the community.

Loserville's local government watchdog group, the CAVE people—Citizens Against Virtually Everything—write editorials pointing out the futility and immorality of the economic development incentives used to attract companies. Corporate welfare must stop, they say.

They call for an immediate moratorium on all incentive programs until a public inquiry into potential abuses can be completed.

Loserville's local news editors exploit the situation knowing it will improve distribution and ratings—at least for that night's broadcast

Phase 12: Blight

Loserville looks bad. If you live there and drive around every day, you might not notice that things are getting worse.

But people who visit every six months or so can really see the steady decline. Favorite local vendors are gone, vacant boarded-up buildings, potholes, weeds and litter are everywhere.

Witnessing the visual decay of a community you live in is psychologically devastating. In addition to the visual evidence of decline, other factors contribute to a sense of blight. The effects of increasing property and violent crime, divorce, drug abuse, poverty and teen pregnancy work on the subconscious minds of every citizen. People start to lose hope. "Maybe I should get my family out of here before it's too late," they say to themselves.

Loserville High hasn't been in the state finals for anything since 1973. It has its share of talented kids, but after a decade of budget cuts, it can't even field full teams in half of the sanctioned extracurricular activities.

When you walk into Loserville High, you see an enormous trophy case that was built and dedicated by the woodshop class of 1956. It looks like an old museum display, and is loaded with tarnished old trophies and dusty, faded banners from the 1940s, 50s and 60s. Instead of inspiring confidence, ambition and school spirit, it's a constant reminder that they peaked as a community a long time ago.

For the foreseeable future, Loserville's population is predicted to continue to grow faster than its economy. Every year, local government institutions, businesses and households have to serve more people with less revenue while adding more debt to the books.

Without the qualified workers and the wealth they generate, the spiral continues. If a major economic base employer shuts down or declines to move there, and the community doesn't find an immediate replacement, it risks losing even more of its dwindling qualified workforce.

Every time a 24-to-44-year-old-qualified worker leaves the community and is replaced by a retiree or an unqualified worker, the hole the community is digging for itself gets a little deeper.

Qualified workers who don't want to leave, or can't, wind up hedging their bets by opting for lower paying, less challenging work with employers or institutions. The end result: a smaller economic base, and a smaller, less capable local labor pool.

As qualified workers, wealthy retirees and college-bound seniors pour out of the community, the only people willing to move in are those with no other choice—poor retirees looking for a bargain, the chronically poor and the criminals who prey on them.

The community's population continues to grow. Local tax receipts may actually increase because the population is continuing to grow. But it's deceiving. Growth in this case is debilitating because it comes with a net increase in the service burden. An ever-growing class of retired dependents and those unqualified to work must be supported by a shrinking proportion of workers able to earn a subsistence wage. The service burden of the community's tax-dependent institutions grows faster than its revenue.

The day it reaches full employment of its qualified workers, economic development essentially ceases. The relentless, unbalanced situation keeps the community's local government and tax-dependent institutions in a perpetual state of financial duress. Local leaders and institution managers spend all their time and energy on the defensive.

With no plan or financing for making the improvements needed to begin attracting and holding more 24-to-44-year-old qualified workers, the community can only appeal to the charity of state and federal governments for help. Since they too are broke, no one is holding their breath.

Pretty soon another economic base employer realizes that it can't get the qualified workers it needs if it is to stay in Loserville. When it starts losing employees and can't replace them, there is no recovery part of the cycle, and the community begins a second spin on the Death Spiral.

It's one thing to endure a recession, and quite another to pull out of one. Poor, inner-city neighborhoods, rust-belt communities, mining towns and agricultural communities have been dealing with chronic contraction conditions for decades. This time, because of demographics, it's going to happen to a new class of communities, and most don't even know they are at risk.

Chapter 11

Winnerville

Sixty miles down the road from Loserville is Winnerville. It has the same number of people and an identical geographic setting. Instead of a death spiral, all key metrics of community quality improve every year, bucking regional and national trends. What separates Winnerville from other places? One thing: people want to live there.

Phase 1: Plentiful Talent

Winnerville has begun to develop a national reputation as a great place to live and work. As a result of being featured frequently in national magazine polls as one of the best places to live, thousands of qualified workers around the country are planning to eventually move there. Winnerville attracts and holds onto more qualified workers every year than it loses.

The number of 24-to-44-year-olds is staying roughly at parity with the 64-to-84-year-old age group. The numbers show that Winnerville attracts enough new qualified workers to more than offset those who leave the workforce or the community. A deeper look reveals that the local demographic churn, combined with an integrated economic and workforce development program, is resulting in a workforce that is larger, better educated, more productive and better aligned with the demands of their economic base and service sector every year.

While it may seem obvious today, Winnerville's business and community leaders saw the threat in the national demographic numbers a decade ago when few others did. They could see that the economic development game was going to change abruptly from a contest for corporate investment to a contest for qualified workers.

They did not need an outside consultant to tell them that their workforce institutions, economic development and business development organizations were uncoordinated and unprepared. They understood that surviving in this new demographic environment would require fixing complex systems and institutions, and that it would not be easy.

Phase 2: Get Predictive Data

They got predictive data, got leadership consensus, came up with a plan and acted decisively to implement it. A team led by the community college board president was convened to plan a complete overhaul of Winnerville's economic development and workforce development strategies and its data analysis functions.

The restructuring focused on three areas: developing a data-driven sense of what was going on, integrating economic development and workforce development efforts, and executing those strategies.

Early on, the Center for Predictive Research was formed to get the predictive data they needed. They then forced the workforce development and economic development program activities into a single organization called the Workforce and Job Creation Organization. Finally, they created an overarching governing council to pass judgment on the performance of the community's economic and workforce institutions.

Maybe the greatest single underlying factor distinguishing Winnerville from other places is that its leaders invest ten times more local public and private money in collecting and analyzing predictive data on the community and its institutions than their peers. Most of this investment goes to fund the Winnerville Center for Predictive Research.

The Center is run by an independent board and is directed by a prominent national economic demographer. It produces predictive data and in-depth reports on the key metrics driving the quality of the community. The Center's staff and their outside contractors are in continuous consultation with the leadership and management of Winnerville's local government jurisdictions and tax-dependent institutions.

The Center's research and conclusions are public, so anyone inside or outside the community can see what's going on. The analytical candor enables leadership, local residents and business owners—and outsiders—to know more about Winnerville's demographic, economic and social conditions and trends than any other place in the country.

As a result, no problem goes undetected, ignored or untreated for long. The community's investment in developing predictive data discourages mischief from the radical elements and special interests, and helps focus the minds of leaders and voters on fixing the big problems. Just as importantly, anyone trying to decide whether to stay, come, or go is able to make a more informed and confident decision.

The converse is also true. When you can't get good comparative data on competing places, it raises questions and creates uncertainty. A footloose qualified worker thinking about moving to (or back to) your community will be increasingly wary of the risks of investing in a place that doesn't collect, analyze or publish honest trend data on itself. Do you want to invest in a place that doesn't know what's going on? There is always the probability that they do know, but they don't want you to know.

In this new world of instant, real-time data, not having data or not publishing it is a major tip-off that something is wrong. In fact, the Winnerville CPR is turning out to be the community's most important tool for recruiting crucial new talent. Now, political incumbents and the chamber of commerce are inclined to suffer the negative consequences of transparency quietly.

Another big difference between Winnerville and Loserville is the editorial quality of their respective news media outlets. In Winnerville, most of the local media outlets are owned or managed by fair-minded people who care about the community and understand how it works.

Reporters and editors are among the best paid in the region. Most have been working in the community for many years and have a deep and nuanced understanding of the subject areas they report on.

There is a spectrum of bloggers and citizen reporters writing informed pieces on all subjects. So information and analysis is diverse, in-depth, analytical and educational.

In addition to establishing the Center for Predictive Research, they recommended merging their local economic development and workforce development organizations. Since workforce was going to be the weak side of the economic development equation from here on out, it was decided that workforce should be put ahead of Job Creation in the organization's new name—the Workforce and Job Creation Organization. Getting everyone to go along with the new organizational structure required heroic leadership and plenty of coercion.

The WJCO, the CPR, the chamber of commerce and the community development foundation each send one delegate to a super council that meets twice a year to pass judgment on the return on the community's investment in these programs, settle any major turf issues and consider new strategies and ideas.

With predictive data from the CPR, the WJCO was able to project the total number of economic base jobs needed to support the economy with the target or assumed population. Factoring for a major shift in the dependency ratio, they were able to extrapolate the projected number of service jobs by sector.

By contrasting future numbers of jobs predicted to be in demand with talent pipeline trends and assumptions, the group was able to predict where the significant gaps in qualified workers would most likely occur.

Winnerville constantly updates the model methodology and the data so students, parents, policymakers and employers can make better decisions about preparing for the future.

There is a general understanding among the community's leaders that thirty percent of the community's discretionary resources will be invested directly into projects, programs and initiatives that directly improve the ecosystem for the community's target economic base industries and build up the pipeline of talent to fill predicted gaps in the workforce.

Phase 3: Loyal Economic Base Employers

Every time one of Winnerville's economic base employers downsized or closed their doors, the community acted quickly to keep laid off workers from leaving. Generous income maintenance incentives were added to the state and federal programs.

One allowed employees of downsizing economic base employers to reduce their hours to half time and receive state and local income maintenance benefits for up to twenty hours a week for a given period of time.

This allowed time for the company to reduce labor costs during slow times without losing valued employees.

Over the years, these workforce preservation tactics by the community have encouraged several of Winnerville's major economic base employers to consolidate their operations there instead of downsizing or closing.

In the cases where the employer did close, the community was able to quickly attract another that paid higher wages.

Phase 4: Service Sector Expansion

The population is growing and increasing the demand for government infrastructure and services from Winnerville's tax-dependent institutions. But unlike Loserville, its local tax receipts are growing faster than the service burden, giving it a little more to work with each year. One of the clearest indicators is the fact that its commercial tax revenue grows a little faster than revenue coming from residential sources.

With the population and the service sector growing every year, demand for locally produced goods and services grows as well. Not only is it getting bigger, it's gaining critical mass. Winnerville shoppers have a little more variety and better pricing every year, resulting in a higher percentage of locally-earned dollars being spent in the community. As the local market for goods and services grows, more residents and employers buy locally, which means a larger tax base.

Since growth in residential tax revenue usually comes with a proportional amount of new service burdens, it's difficult for a community to get ahead. A community's economy is improving when tax revenue from commercial tax sources consistently grow at a faster rate than those from residential sources. It's a clear sign that the economy is growing faster than the population.

Another positive sign for Winnerville is that local government expenditures as a percentage of per capita income ranks among the lowest in the region. Residents' and companies' net worth is growing faster than tax receipts.

Phase 5: Net Worth Increasing

More spending is being done in town, so revenue per square foot is going up at local stores. This drives up the value of local business locations and their assessed valuation for property tax purposes. The value of retail and commercial real estate is in large part a function of sales per square foot. The more sales per square foot, the more that location (land and building) is worth.

Phase 6: Tax Base Expands

With the extra earnings, local businesses are able to invest in new technology and training, which makes their employees more productive. Local service sector wages rise, helping to drive up household earnings and net worth. As Winnerville's commercial sales per square foot increases, property taxes and gross receipts taxes rise. In this scenario, they rise faster than the service burden of Winnerville's tax-dependent institutions. With service sector businesses doing better every year, owners, managers and employees earn more and keep more. They invest more in improving their homes, their health, and their education. They buy energy-efficient cars and appliances. In the end, they invest more in improving the community. The community gets even better, becoming even more attractive.

Phase 7: Cost Control and Investment

Even while federal and state tax rates have gone up, Winnerville's tax-dependent institutions have been able to hold the line. In addition to having a little more revenue from steady net economic growth, they have been strategically investing their discretionary resources in the technology, training and preventative maintenance needed to reduce costs and operate more efficiently.

The tax base is growing faster than the service burden. Cha-Ching! They have more discretionary resources to invest in making Winnerville even nicer.

Winnerville High teams are reigning state champions in both girls' and boys' basketball, and they are perennial contenders in all the minor sports. They also dominate in the nerd sports of science fairs, debating and music, to the point it is making it difficult for state organizers to call them contests.

Entering Winnerville High you are greeted by a gallery of personal profiles showcasing its most successful grads in the areas of science, business, education, the arts and sports. New profiles are added every month, and the message is clear: We make winners here and we expect your picture to be up there in a few years.

A carrot-and-stick approach applied to students, parents, teachers and administrators has simultaneously brought Winnerville's dropout rate down from eighteen percent to seven percent, and elevated test scores at every grade level to the best in the region. Per capita teen pregnancy, drug use and juvenile crime have seen similar declines.

The high school, community college and all local workforce development and labor institutions administer Work Keys tests (an evaluation tool that gauges a person's level of preparation for a specific job) for admission, and as the threshold for workplace readiness.

Every elementary, middle and high school in Winnerville is operating well above the national standard, and at this point, the community's expectations are so high that they would be horrified if one didn't.

The high school and community college have reputations for being far superior to anything in the region for producing local talent ready to work. Some national companies are sending their human resource scouts and headhunters to Winnerville High School and community college career fairs to look for talent. And when they do, they have to compete with a host of Winnerville's economic base and service sector employers.

Winnerville High, the community college and local employers have been working and investing strategically to develop a pipeline of local talent. Economic base employers in the community's five target industry sectors are collaborating to create apprenticeship programs, mentoring relationships and work-study opportunities for students. Even more importantly, they are providing sabbatical and summer employment positions for teachers and administrators.

As a result, the schools are attracting and retaining a better class of teachers and administrators, and the community's economic base employers are able to build a bigger and better pool of qualified workers.

The Winnerville CPR produces an annual report showing the biggest gaps in the supply of qualified workers at the national, regional and local level. This data is published annually for local school and workforce development counselors, parents, teachers and administrators.

Winnerville students are encouraged to declare or confirm an after-high-school career destination every two years. The high school has apprenticeship and college preparatory programs for all students. Winnerville high and middle schools are open six days a week, 7 a.m. to 5 p.m. Truancy is a class-one misdemeanor, and parents who fail to get their kids to school and prepared to learn, are counseled and ultimately fined. Admission to charter schools comes with random drug testing from eighth grade on.

The citizens of Winnerville tax themselves one percent a year to generate a college tuition fund for the poorest students in each graduating class. Local businesses, service groups and religious organizations raise matching funds for room and board.

The Winnerville Community College was one of the first community colleges in the country to establish a formal marketing department. The department works closely with local employers and the Winnerville CPR to adjust the scale and alignment of its instructional programs to match the predicted needs of the economic base. For example, the center is predicting serious gaps in the supply of accounting, IT and nurse practitioners, so programs in those areas have been increased. Screening is done to identify smart, ambitious students and mid-career change candidates. A psychological profile is being developed for predicting which students and workers are most likely to remain in the area, or return to live and work.

Winnerville's service clubs have all adopted rules that require members over fifty years old to recruit and maintain two new members under forty to stay in the club. The number and size of clubs has tripled in the last five years.

Winnervilles's chronic prosperity is even more conspicuous in contrast to its rival down the road. Longtime residents of both towns, and outside observers, have a wide range of opinions about how two seemingly similar places could be on such different trajectories. The two towns face the same national economic, demographic and social conditions. Why is one winning and the other losing? Is it luck or leadership?

What you really want to know is whether you're living in a Winnerville or Loserville. Or are you on the bubble?

Part Four

Predict, Think and Innovate

OPERATIONAL DEFINITION OF ECONOMIC DEVELOPMENT

E = Economy | P = Population

Chapter 12

Predicting Winners and Losers

"Not everything that counts can be counted, and not everything that can be counted counts."—Sign hanging in Albert Einstein's office at Princeton

Not sure where your community is headed? It's like gauging your health. It starts with a self exam—one with a heightened awareness of the realities ahead. If your self-exam leaves you concerned, then you will want to schedule a checkup. To be sure, you can always invest in a Mayo Clinic-style full diagnostic round of tests.

If that turns up major issues, then you'll need to start seeing some specialists. When you are done, you will likely be faced with a range of solutions. Here is a protocol for diagnosing your community's risk of entering an economic death spiral and becoming a loser.

Need to be Somewhere Else?

Ask yourself: Is there a community within seven hundred and fifty miles where you would rather live? Assume someone is covering the moving costs and you will have the same job. Is your community going to remain attractive enough to steal qualified workers at will from other places and hold onto them? If you really like where you are and the community is a talent magnet, then you can stop here. Conversely, if you are dreaming of leaving and think the community is doomed, you do not have to go any further. Call a realtor and start packing.

Not sure? You'll have to go a little deeper.

Pass/Fail Report Card

You have to be able to educate, train and hold onto enough qualified workers to balance the economy's dependents. Few will be able. Meaning, if you can't attract and train more talent than you lose every year, you run the risk of entering a death spiral. So how do you tell?

There are six metrics that make up this self-administered exam.

1. **Economy** - The local economy is growing faster than the population and is becoming more diverse.
2. **Population** - Qualified workers and dependents too young to work are growing in proportion to unqualified workers and those too old to work.
3. **Ecosystem** - The environment is improving and natural resource base is adequate and improving.
4. **Education** - The K-20 education system is improving and more aligned with the needs of local employers.
5. **Crime** - The community is getting safer and more honest? Corruption, violent and property crime are low and declining.
6. **Housing** - Workers earning 1.5 times the poverty rate can afford to rent or own a home.
7. **Health care** - Access and quality of health care services are good and improving?

For each of the six metrics you are asked to make three judgment calls: past, present and future.

Past - Has the general quality direction of each metric improved or declined over the last seven years?

Present - Do you consider the level of quality today to be a net advantage or disadvantage to the quality of life in the community?

Future - Do you expect the level of quality to substantially improve in the next seven years or get worse?

You should be able to answer these questions quickly without looking at any data. Try to answer them intuitively. If you find yourself having trouble with an up-or-down call on any of these, you can jump ahead a few pages and run through a deeper, more detailed list of factors that indicate how a community is doing in each area.

In this report card exercise, though, you must choose either better or worse for past and future and either satisfactory, or unsatisfactory for present condition. "Don't know" or "no change" is not an acceptable answer. You have to circle a (+) or a (-). Make the call and circle the plus or the minus for each category, past, present and future. Then add up the scores.

Community Quality Report Card

Factor	Past	Present	Future	Cumulative
Population	+ /-	+/-	+/-	+3 to -3
Economy	+ /-	+/-	+/-	+3 to -3
Ecosystem	+ /-	+/-	+/-	+3 to -3
Education	+ /-	+/-	+/-	+3 to -3
Crime	+ /-	+/-	+/-	+3 to -3
Housing	+ /-	+/-	+/-	+3 to -3
Healthcare	+/-	+/-	+/-	+3 to -3
Total Score				+21 to -21

The maximum score for any single metric is +3. The maximum total score over all 6 metrics is +21. If you have a score of -2 or -3 for any row (factor), you have a serious problem. If you have a total score of less than +10, your community is at risk and you should seriously consider an expanded diagnostic.

Below is a list of metrics that can be used to identify the hot spots threatening the viability of your community.

Winner/Loser Diagnostic

Generally Positive	**Generally Negative**
Population	
Population is growing	Shrinking
Pop growing, with educated, high net worth, people	Poor uneducated?
Fertility rate is 2.5 or higher	Below 2.5
Net gain is from high birth rate of middle class	Poor uneducated
Population becoming more diverse	Less diverse
Population becoming more tolerant	Less tolerant
Dependency ratio is stable or improving	Worsening
24-44 cohort growing faster than 45-84 cohort	45-84 growing faster
Workforce	
Workforce growing faster than the population	Slower
Qualified Workforce growing faster than population	Slower
Productivity increasing faster than nation	Slower
Qualified workers exceed 35% of population	Less than 35%
% of qualified workers increasing	Decreasing
Age distribution of workforce skewing younger	Skewing older
Local skills supply matches demand	Skills mismatch
Gaining qualified workers faster than losing	Losing
Unemployment rate above 4 % and below 6 %	Below 4% / above 6%
Low turnover – low transience	High turnover
High rate of job acceptance	Low rate
Business community involved in local schools	Relatively uninvolved
Skills gaps projections used to shape curriculum	Not used
Brain gain	Brain drain
Workforce gaps filling	Widening
Diversity increasing	Decreasing
More people want to come than want to leave	More want to leave
Pre-employment Pipeline Development	
High school dropout rate falling	Rising
Business community engaged in local schools	Business uninvolved
Skills gaps projections used to shape curriculum	Not used
Mid-Career Candidate Development	
Mid-career change strategy to fill gaps in place	None
Post-secondary enrollment in target programs rising	Falling
Local labor gap market data driving college resource allocations	No market data use
Local Economy	
Economy growing faster than the population	Slower
Commercial tax base growing faster than residential	Residential grows faster

Per capita income growing faster than inflation	Slower
Household income growing faster than inflation	Slower
Business climate competitive	Uncompetitive
Business climate improving	Declining
Commute burden 18 minutes or lower	20 minutes or higher
Government service burden low and falling	High and rising
Economic Base	
Economic base output rising	Falling
Economic base jobs growing faster than population	Slower
Economic base job wages rising faster than inflation	Slower
Economic base jobs high value sectors growing in %	Shrinking
Economic base more diverse	Less
Major economic base sectors relatively secure	At risk
Economic base in proportion to local workforce	Bedroom community
Economic base firms not at risk to retirement	At risk
Capacity utilization in acceptable range	Too high or too low
Benefits packages improving	Declining
Service Sector	
Service sector jobs growing faster than population	Slower
Range and spectrum of local services improving	Declining
Leakage decreasing	Increasing
Per capita gross receipts rising	Falling
Revenue per square foot of retail business rising	Falling
Gross receipts from new construction under 15%	Over 15%
Net Worth	
Home equity rising	Falling
Home equity above national average	Below
Savings above national average & rising	Below and falling
Home sales (mobility) higher than national average	Low
Percentage of population below poverty rate falling	Rising
School lunch program enrollment falling	Rising
Per capita government transfer payments falling	Rising
Ecosystem	
Air quality good and improving	Degrading
Water quality and supply good and improving	Depleting/degrading
Sources of pollution understood and mitigated	Neglected
Relatively free of natural disasters – climate change	At risk
Environmental disease decreasing	Increasing
Education	
Early childhood programs supported	Neglected
At risk pre-school programs supported	Neglected
Test scores rising	Falling
Schools exceeding compliance standards rising	30% failing
SAT & Work Keys scores rising	Falling
HS Tech vocational programs supported	Neglected
Crime	
Personal violent crime is low and falling	High and rising
Property crime is low and falling	High and rising

Teen delinquency low and falling	High and rising
Drug use is low and falling	High and rising
Uninsured motorists low and falling	High and rising
Political corruption low and falling	High and rising
Housing	
Site-built home ownership over 60% and rising	Under 60% & falling
Supply of housing in balance with demand	Shortage or glut
Supply of workforce housing adequate	Shortage
Cost of housing is moderate	Too high or low
Home value appreciating	Values falling
Home values relatively stable	Values rising fast
Healthcare	
Hospitals quality and availability good and rising	Absent, bad or falling
No health care professional shortages	Shortages
Emergency room visits declining	Increasing
Childhood obesity declining	Increasing
Uninsured claims decreasing	Increasing

Obviously this checklist is admittedly both incomplete and arbitrary. Some major factors related to energy, telecommunications, transportation and food security did not make this list. So add or subtract categories or standards as you see fit. Just make sure you have a way to measure it.

Existing Data Analytics

There are a wide range of metrics that can be used to measure how well a community is doing economically. Don't put too much stock in rankings and comparisons published every year by magazines and foundations. They are almost all trying to sell you something.

It is more important to track quarterly and yearly changes and monitor trends in metrics that are important to your survival. Some of the most common and useful metrics are presented below.

Gross domestic product (GDP) is the total market value of all goods and services produced within the community within a given period of time (usually a calendar year). This is a calculated figure, based on:

Household expenditures
Household equity gains; savings, pensions & home equity
Capital investment by businesses or households
Government expenditures
Gross exports
Gross imports

Changes in the **number of jobs and average salaries** are also often used as a measure of economic growth, particularly when the community has a high unemployment rate, and therefore many people needing jobs.

Changes in **the number of economic base jobs and the average salaries in each economic base sector** is crucial information that is rarely collected or analyzed at the community level. This tells a community whether its economic base is growing, and allows economists to calculate economic base job service multipliers.

Changes in **average personal and household income** can also serve as a metric for economics on the individual level. Productivity metrics can indicate whether economic growth is occurring as a result of increases in productivity.

Changes in **the unemployment rate** measures the percentage of people actively seeking employment within the last four weeks who are not working. This does not measure people who could be in the labor force but who are not interested in working, such as retirees, full-time parents, students or people who have given up looking for work.

Changes in **underemployment** measure the number of people who are working at jobs for which they are overqualified, or those who cannot find employment in the field for which they are trained. The mismatch usually means that local residents are not as productive as they could be, and it's a sign that the community has a hidden workforce that might be attractive to employers.

Changes in local **poverty rates** measure how much money families have for housing, food, and other expenses. Rates are developed by the U.S. Census Bureau and vary depending on the number of people in the household and change annually. For example, the 2006 poverty level for a person under sixty-five years old was $10,488.

Changes in **labor participation** measures changes in the percentage of the working-age population that are actually working. Labor participation is important because it reveals how many people are left in the workforce. Rising labor participation, especially of women and retirement-age residents coinciding with a falling unemployment rate is a clear sign the community is running out of labor.

Changes in **capacity utilization** measures the amount of capital equipment, buildings and skilled labor left idle in the economy. Falling capacity utilization means that the community has an idle productive capacity that could be used to grow the economy without major new investment.

Changes in **local tax burden per household** and per capita can indicate whether the community's tax receipts are staying in balance with municipal, county and school district service burdens. A growing imbalance can be a sign that the community's economy (tax base) is shrinking in proportion to population.

Changes in **the ratio of commercial to residential sources** of local tax revenue can help reveal whether the economy is growing faster than the population. Residential tax revenue usually grows proportionally with the local government service burden, so if commercial revenue is growing faster, it's a sign of economic development.

Changes in **personal property valuations** measures increases or decreases in the net worth of people living in the community. Major trends in, or changes in the equity value of local real estate, 401(k)s and/or pensions of local residents will eventually affect the community's economic performance.

Changes in the **dependency ratio** compares the number of working people to those too young or too old to work. A negative ratio means that there are more people in the community out of the workforce A steadily rising dependency ratio means that working residents are supporting more non-working residents every year.

Getting Predictive Data

What we are going to need are predictive data, especially for communities on the bubble. People running institutions need numbers in order to make and defend decisions. Measuring this stuff takes time and money. Figure out the essentials and measure changes. What you measure tells people about your priorities.

Getting predictive data to populate these graphs is going to be harder than you think. Most of the people doing this kind of analysis for communities have been doing it for a long time. While they often have slightly different methodologies, they rely on data sets that were developed to understand and measure a 1940s-era economy.

The best way for a community to get the predictive and comparative data needed to figure out what's really happening there is to hire an economic demographer.

If you asked me what the single most important thing a community can do to prepare for the realities of the coming zero-sum labor market, I would say hire a couple of the best economic demographers in the country, move them to your community and fund them to develop a predictive data program.

It won't be easy. It won't be popular. And it won't be cheap. You'll need to make sure you have a good handle on the program of work before you write the request for proposal and start interviewing. You will be asking them to develop a number of diagnostic sets.

Tell them what you want measured and how you want the data displayed. Some of what you need, they will be able to get by mining and manipulating existing data sets. Some they may be able to get by doing regular surveys and polls. But for some of the really important stuff, they will need to design, develop and collect new data.

New Diagnostics Needed
Population, Workforce Shift Analysis

What we are after here is a snapshot of where the population side of the community's E > P formula is at.

Population growth: You want to know how many people are going to be living in your community. You want to know how many will be net contributors compared to dependents. You want to try and predict changes in the following four quadrants of your population over time:

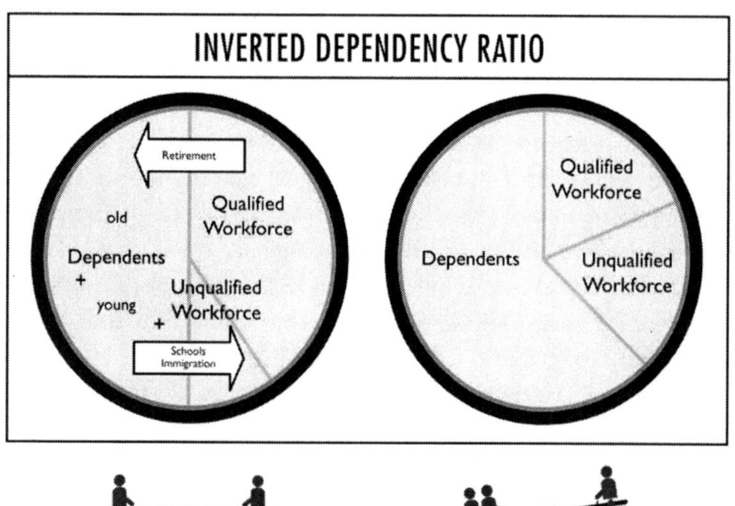

1 Dependent : 1 Worker

2 Dependents : 1 Worker

Too old to work or disabled
Too young to work
Not qualified - earns under 1.5 times the poverty rate
Qualified - earns over 1.5 percent of poverty rate

At the self-exam level, you can just estimate whether you think each sector of the Population Dependency pie chart will grow or shrink during the next seven years. This exercise should indicate whether your community is a death spiral candidate or not. Death spiral candidates will have rapidly growing "dependent" and "not qualified" quadrants, while the proportion of "qualified workers" shrinks.

An Economic Base Analysis

What industry sectors make up your community's economic base? Which are shrinking, which are growing, which are becoming more productive, which are at risk and which new ones should you consider going after?

A **net worth survey and local equity tracking model** monitors changes in the liquid net worth of local businesses and households.

A **workers-to-geezers projection** will tell you the number of 24-to-44-year-olds in the community compared to the number of 64-to-84-year-olds. If the older group is projected to grow twice as fast as the younger one over the next decade, you should be concerned.

An **age distribution risk analysis of economic base employers** surveys key local economic base employers for the risk that high rates of retirement in the years ahead could have on the viability of key employers. Early diagnoses of these problems are the key to solving them.

A **jobs/workforce gap analysis** methodology needs to be developed that would enable communities to predict and quantify significant gaps in the supply of qualified workers needed to staff the economy. This analysis would help draw local talent into the career paths that the economy needs to keep growing.

A workforce map should be built by using statistical polling methodologies and **Work Keys. A pre-employment pipeline** tracking system should be developed that gathers current data on students and mid-career change candidates with the specific education and skills needed for key employment sectors.

A **workforce housing demand model** that predicts the demand for new housing based on demographic and employment assumptions will be needed in many communities if they are to avoid being starved of new workers.

If we don't get way more data than we have now, we simply won't know enough about what is going on in our communities to take the corrective action in time to keep us out of trouble. Even if we see the problems coming, there is the matter of what to do about them.

Chapter 13

Thinking and Innovating

Initially, I had ruled out trying to cover what to do in this book. I had my hands full trying to understand all the dimensions of this new paradigm and their consequences. It seemed a little premature to be telling people what new approaches, products and programs solutions to use when I didn't understand it very well and I didn't know how to measure it. I was just beginning to learn that much of what we had been doing was not going to work in a market chronically starved of labor and capital.

Besides, most of the things on a "What to Do List" depend on who you are, where you live and on what part of the problem you want to focus.

I changed my mind for a couple of reasons. When I first started giving my "The End of Economic Development" speech at national conferences, my message was not very upbeat. In fact, it was so depressing that I was being introduced as the Dr. Kevorkian of economic development.

It was my wife Mary Anne who pointed out that there is no virtue in telling someone they are screwed when there is nothing they can do about it. It's cruel to bring up big scary problems like the demise of someone's profession or their hometown and not leave them with ideas on how to fix them.

The other thing that changed my mind was that by the

time I got to this point in the book, a think tank we had started to work on these issues had begun to come up with some ideas. A few have developed to the point where they are promising enough to talk about.

So I want to do some things in this chapter. First, present some insight we have gained on how to organize thinking and stir innovation around this subject. Second, I want to share some of the ideas that we've come up with so far.

By 2004, a small group of us were meeting several times a year to talk about the impact labor scarcity was having on economic development. At first we were an ad hoc group meeting occasionally, sharing papers, articles, studies and insights on the subject.

The group's members were mostly renegade thinkers from a variety of disciplines from all over the U.S. and Canada. We had economic developers, economists, demographers, physicists, bankers, site-selection consultants, urban planners, real estate developers, workforce developers and a school system superintendent.

As the U.S. economy overheated on the way to the Great Recession, we could see clear evidence that many places were out of labor, and thereby out of the economic development game. We were focused on two things: a better understanding of how zero-sum labor markets might change the economic development game, and finding some new big ideas to test.

In 2008, we incorporated the Community Economics Lab (CELab) as a private, not-for-profit. The mission: find new ways to do economic development in labor-and-capital-constrained economies. The process we adopted uses four steps: 1. Think Tank to, 2. White Paper to, 3. Pilot Program to, 4. Proliferation.

Some of us saw it as an economic development version of the Manhattan Project. A bunch of us huddled up in New Mexico, periodically trying to come up with practical solutions to this wicked problem—one that many of us believe is one of greatest threats to our national security and well being.

Dealing with Wicked Problems

Complex problems like this are called wicked problems. You cannot rely on linear or reductionist analytical approaches alone when you are dealing with complex problems.

While it's productive to drill down into the subcomponents of wicked problems, they usually can't be solved that way. They require a systems fix, and most of the time it's a system that doesn't want to be fixed.

One technique we use involves pulling back from looking at sub-elements of a problem to looking at it in all of its glorious complexity. As President Dwight Eisenhower once said, "If a problem cannot be solved, enlarge it." When we pull back out to thirty thousand feet and put one or two other unrelated wicked problems on the white board with it, the discussion broadens, the group starts associating aspects of one to another. This associative thinking often results in a whole new round of ideas being generated.

This process of pulling away from a micro-focus on a problem, embracing the complexity of it all, and shoving a couple of other big hairy problems into the mix has triggered most of our breakthrough moments. Sometimes it's hard to get started, and you need the right intellectual chemistry, but when it works, it's magic.

Our lab group vowed to work only on ideas that were new, untested and potentially transformational. We tried to stay away from ideas or projects that made incremental improvements to traditional program approaches.

One of this paradigm dilemma is that there are too many aspects of the problem and too many perspectives to track.

You can't think about or work on all the different aspects of the problem at once, nor can you look at the problem from every perspective. You need a system to deal with the system. You need a way to discipline deliberations so you can park ideas, issues and insights and keep track of them. And you need a systematic way to check different perspectives. You need a way to think about it.

Remember the population pie chart in Chapter 7? It had four quadrants: 1. Too old to work, 2. Too young to work, 3. Unqualified workers, and 4. Qualified workers. We also call it the Community Population Life Cycle and we use it to discipline discussions and keep track of the insights and new ideas generated. It also serves as a constant reminder of how big and complex this problem really is. If you think about it, every factor and force associated with the problem can be plotted on the Community Population Life Cycle chart.

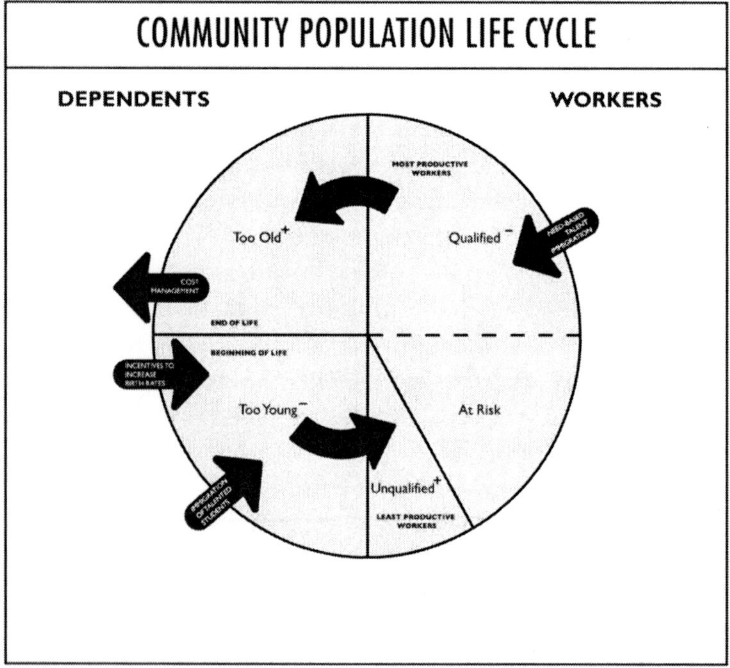

Each quadrant or piece of the pie has three sides or frontiers. At the perimeter you will find the vectors or forces acting on the problem from outside. Along the two sides bordering the neighboring quadrants, you will find the forces and factors related to the neighboring quadrants.

You will find a diagram showing the list of forces, vectors and issues present at the border of each quadrant.

Each boundary represents a frontier of the problem. These frontiers are where innovation and reform will happen. This applies whether you are focused on the national, regional or local economy.

For example, let's take the qualified-worker quadrant. At the twelve o'clock position in the pie chart, there is a frontier between the qualified-workers quadrant and the too-old-to-work quadrant. Here, the most qualified and productive workers in the economy, the Boomers, are moving across into the dependent and too-old-to-work side of the population. This is a frontier that accounts for a big part of the problem. It's an area in need of significant innovation.

This frontier begs the question: what do we have to do to keep Boomers on the job and producing at peak levels?

Here we find everything from neuro-systems engineering and preventive health approaches that keep aging brains operating at peak efficiency longer, to changes we might make in tax codes, labor law and zoning regulations that might encourage older workers to stay in the workforce.

A lot of research has already been done on understanding the differences in the way Boomers and younger generations approach work and life. It's a major problem for corporate employers, and solving it will be crucial if we are to keep Boomers working.

Developers and city planners need to think about hybrid housing complexes that provide the retirement lifestyle amenities for Boomers so they can wind down a little and get the health maintenance they need while providing the ecosystem amenities they need to keep working. How we manage health care, housing and tax policy in the near future will have a major impact on how many seniors stay in the workforce.

At the same point on the wheel, there are forces pushing the other way. For example, what do you do with the unproductive Boomers who use seniority rules and politics to hang on way past their usefulness? They deprive institutions and enterprises of the new blood needed to boost productivity, and frustrate and delay the development of bright, capable, younger workers.

On the outside perimeter of the qualified-worker quadrant is where the nation, region or community is gaining and losing qualified workers. The movement of qualified workers in and out of the country or community is going to be a critical dynamic to measure and manage. If qualified workers are leaving the community to work somewhere else, and they're leaving faster and in greater numbers than new qualified workers are coming in, then you have a problem. What things do you need to do as a community to become attractive to qualified workers?

On a national level, this frontier is where we deal with an important part of immigration policy. Should we open up Ellis Island again and fast-track citizenship for engineers and medical practitioners? At some point, we probably should.

I think it's a mistake to continue believing that qualified workers in other countries will want to move here and become Americans. We should be worrying about how we are going to keep other countries from stealing our talent in the decades ahead. I know my kids would be tempted to work in Prague or Singapore if they had a chance. At some point, they will have the chance. What can we do to convince our qualified younger workers to stay in our country and in our respective communities?

At five o'clock on the pie chart is the frontier between qualified workers and unqualified workers. This is an area that deserves special scrutiny. A lot of money is already being invested in workforce development and education, but much of it is being squandered.

Other forces are working in both directions. Creative destruction and forces of globalization are bound to continue destroying economic base jobs every year. The jobs that remain, and the new ones being created, will require new and different skills. This has the effect of moving huge numbers of workers from the qualified quadrant of a community's population to the unqualified quadrant. Work that pays a living wage is going to continue to grow more complex and demanding over time. Right now, workforce development institutions are running behind and running blind.

Predicting the jobs that are going to be in demand and the education and skills necessary to do the work is one area in which we need to get better. On the supply side we need to get better at identifying mid-career change candidates and inspire them to invest in training that will match them to the new jobs. Right now, everyone is running blind—including students and mid-career candidates.

Program Approaches

Ultimately, you must work any solution into a program approach or policy. Community approaches to economic development range from highly programmed economic architecture efforts where the community endeavors to design a specific future economy and strategically invests to cause it to develop, to the purely organic approach which relies on the market to reward communities that do a good job of protecting their environmental, cultural and natural resources while efficiently providing quality public infrastructure, education, health and social services.

Process is Everything

When and if you decide to try and tackle these problems you are going to need a process. Taking a diverse group of competing interests, many with diametrically opposed worldviews, through deliberations requires a process. These problems are way too complicated, controversial and important to be winging it.

That said, there currently is no process, at least one that

has been developed, vetted and sanctioned by the economic development profession. Walking a group of community leaders through their economic predicament, setting goals, sorting out and vetting options and coming up with consensus and commitment to an actionable plan is a tricky business. As a result, most community groups end up using the traditional SWOT approach (strengths, weaknesses, opportunities and threats), or borrowing a process from another field.

I've perfected my own process. It's pretty rigid and a little dictatorial, and I've used and perfected it over the years. I didn't mean for it to be a 12-step program, but it is. In many cases it feels like an intervention. In fact, I'm convinced that many communities have little or no chance of overhauling their programs for what is ahead if they don't adhere to this process or something very close to it. Skipping steps or doing them in a different order almost always leads to a fatally flawed or incomplete result.

The 12-Step Program

1. Get the right players
2. Agree to the process and nomenclature
3. Get a data-driven sense of reality
4. Agree on your predicament and needs
5. Choose economic and demographic destinations
6. Target criteria and menu development
7. Target evaluation & verification
8. Develop Metrics transactions/jobs/investment
9. Plan
   a. Marketing and sales
   b. Infrastructure and facilities
   c. Workforce development
   d. Business climate improvement
10. Organization
   a. Mission division - delegation
   b. Governance, structure and accountability

c. Fundraising
11. Hiring
12. Execution and management

You are going to need a guide, too, someone who has been where you want to go. Trying to work through a community's economic development agenda using a business leadership consultant that has never scoped, planned and run a successful economic development effort is like asking your scuba instructor to lead your team on an ascent of Mt. Everest. You are almost guaranteed to fail. There are plenty of experienced people in the economic development field today, but no one is using a proven process. Even the smartest, most experienced economic developer needs to use a process.

In Chapter 6 we outlined the ways to work the economy side of the E > P equation. It's at least a good place to start.

Ways to Manage the Economy Side of E > P

1. Grow the economic base and/or
2. Grow the service sector (reduce leakage)
3. Increase new worth

Growing the economic base only happens six ways:

1. Increase the total number of economic base jobs
2. Grow high-value economic base sectors and/or attrition of low value sectors
3. Increase productivity of your economic base workers, which increases wages
4. Increase number of wealthy retirees
5. Increase the value of government transfer payments
6. Wait for windfall events like spikes in uranium and natural gas prices

Expanding the service sector only happens four ways:

1. Increase the range of goods and services offered
2. Increase the quality of goods and services
3. Reduce the costs (prices) of local services & cost of living
4. Increase the productivity of service sector workers

Increasing net worth only happens four ways:

1. Raise rate of home ownership
2. Raise home value & appreciation
3. Windfall investment returns
4. Raise value of locally-owned assets

Ways to Manage the Population Side of E > P. There are a number of things a community might do to manage the population side of the E > P equation.

1. Improve the dependency ratio
2. Manage the housing supply
3. Fix the school system
4. Retrain mid-career candidates
5. Increase labor participation rates
6. Better matching of employers and workers
7. Attract talent faster

New Approaches, Programs and Solutions

One of the most promising new economic development program ideas produced by the Community Economics Lab is the **Home Based Worker Program**. We nicknamed it the Third Bedroom program because it shifts the focus of local economic base job creation programs from corporate employers, office buildings and industrial parks to the individual workers working from third bedrooms (offices) in their homes.

The idea of creating new jobs one at a time originated from a linear approach to the problem of a steadily tightening labor market.

Site selectors were telling us that our labor market was on the verge of being too tight for them to recommend our location to their clients that were looking for new locations. After looking at the long-term demographic trends and a regional unemployment rate that had dropped from 3.8 to 3.3 percent in the previous year, we figured we had better start looking at recalibrating our industry recruiting program to smaller sized deals.

During one brainstorming session I made three columns on the dry erase board. In the upper left hand corner I put 1,000-job deals. Next to it I put 100-job deals, and to the right, 10-job deals. There was just enough room across the top of the board to put a fourth column headed with one job.

As I put the number one up there, it hit me: There are a lot of people working from home and exporting what they do. Why aren't we counting them as economic base jobs?

Mesa del Sol's goal of building six hundred new homes a year required the creation of four hundred net new economic base jobs each year. Why can't we develop a marketing and sales effort to attract out-of-state home buyers that work from home? As long as the revenue they earn comes from out of state they should qualify as economic base jobs.

The Home Based Work Program Strategy

There were some communities acknowledging the trend of location-neutral work, also referred to as Lone Eagles, but we could not find anyone in the country that had perfected a program platform for recruiting, expanding or starting up solitary home-based economic base jobs.

We knew if we could figure out how to put the strategy on a program footing, it could put a lot of communities back in the economic development game. This approach will work in communities where traditional, employer-focused approaches are limited by a lack of capital, labor, transportation, land, buildings or other shortcomings. It provides local leaders three program strategies for creating high-paying economic base jobs for a fraction of the cost, risk and impacts associated with traditional corporate-focused economic development efforts.

The program uses the same program architecture employed by traditional economic development programs: attraction, expansion and retention, and startup. The difference is that the targets are workers who work alone from a home office, garage, workshop or studio instead of a traditional corporate office or factory.

Home Based Workers can be sole proprietors with their own LLC or S corporations. Some are 1099 contract employees, and others are employees of corporations that are allowed to work primarily from home. The types of work performed by Home Based Workers is expanding every day and includes consultants, writers, artists, digital animators, financial advisors, accountants, graphic designers, medical transcriptions, IT experts and more.

As long as the products or services being produced are billed to customers outside the community, the work is bringing new money into the community and making the local economy bigger. The Home Based Worker sector may be the largest, fastest growing, most lucrative source of footloose economic base jobs, and no one is systematically going after them.

The Home Based Worker economic development strategies being developed by the Community Economics Lab have some compelling advantages compared to traditional economic development approaches.

They are scalable, measurable and bring new allies and partners to the table. Program efforts can be customized to meet the economic needs and cultural sensitivities of any community or region. The jobs created have a minimal impact on the local traffic grid, and they eliminate the need for building, financing, and heating and cooling big office and industrial facilities.

Under the program, community leaders project the number of new economic base jobs they want to create by attracting, expanding or starting up companies over the coming two years. Then we work through projections of new economic base jobs that could be produced using a Home Based Worker program.

The bottom line is these high-value jobs can be created fast in any sized community with a fraction of the community investment associated with traditional economic development programs.

Given the economic conditions likely to persist post-recession, and the long-term demographic realities facing communities, we believe many communities will find this a practical alternative to traditional economic development program approaches. The fact that this class of economic base activity is currently ignored by state and local economic development organizations means there is virtually no competition—for the moment.

We came up with some innovative ideas such as a community supported **Geek Squad** of priority support IT and business services. We also designed a **Shared Service Platform** concept that features a physical location where participating home-based workers could use meeting space and avail themselves to a suite of discounted business services. These shared services sites also double as informal, third-place gathering spaces for the community's most creative workers. In the end, we didn't think these amenities would be enough to get the majority of the community's home-based workers to show themselves or compel an out-of-state candidate to move. We needed something else.

The other big obstacle was the operating, or transaction costs, associated with promoting, screening, supporting and measuring the program. We needed an automated system where a maximum number of individuals could find the program, get their questions answered and become qualified for the benefits of participation. The ultimate solution is the development of an online community model.

Following is a sample of some program ideas being developed at the Community Economics Lab:

Jobs/housing balance policy innovations that encourage or require residential developers to provide for and commit to specific job creation thresholds in exchange for entitlements. Besides taking commuters off the local traffic grid, home-based worker thresholds will increase the demand for commercial and retail activity.

Hybrid housing strategies designed to keep aging Boomers healthier, more active, sharper, and working longer.

Merchant economic development services group is a new business model that privatizes traditional economic development services for a consortia of communities that wish to share sub-contracted economic development services for marketing, sales and project development.

Gradually retiring federal worker programs that cater to and support clusters of gradually retiring federal workers whose agencies still need them.

A workforce mapping and matching program that provides employers, students, mid-career change candidates, the unemployed, education and training institutions and local labor departments and placement offices with data on immediate and projected job demand.

The program is also used to help communities identify transferable skills in their workforce for the purpose of choosing new industry targets.

One thing is for sure, no community is going to exert influence over its current economic development path by pouring more resources into approaches and programs that have been producing diminishing returns. We are going to have to innovate and execute like our lives depend on it, because they do.

Why this is Important

The Story of Mrs. Griego

Creating good-paying jobs is beyond important. It means survival, life, purpose, dignity, and identity for every person in your community and in this country. Whatever our priorities, life isn't much without a good job.

Economists make charts and graphs, politicians drone on and on about jobs, and pundits pontificate from the comfort of their dens or newsrooms.

In the end, when we talk about economic development, we're talking about people's lives.

Here's a story that hammered home to me the reason economic development is important and worth doing, and doing right.

It was 1983. I had just finished my second interview for what would be my first economic development job. I was in Grants, New Mexico, which was in serious economic trouble. Following the accident at the Three Mile Island nuclear power plant in March, 1979, near Harrisburg, Pennsylvania, more than one hundred new nuclear power plant projects had been canceled across the United States. The Grants area's economy had been decimated by the collapse of the uranium industry.

Within eighteen months of the disaster, the uranium mines and mills around Grants, which amounted to about sixty percent of the area's economic base, had been shut down. Layoffs were massive.

Grants had been a small, classic, boom-bust mining town seventy miles west of Albuquerque. Since the early 1960s, Grants had been the primary source of the nation's uranium ore—first for our nuclear weapons program, and later for the nuclear power industry. Now Grants was in trouble.

Suddenly, more than eight thousand people were out of work. More than thirty industrial buildings stood vacant. Banks were in trouble, stores were closing, trucks were for sale on every corner and houses were boarded up and for sale everywhere.

Following a series of meetings with the board of the newly-formed Greater Grants Industrial Development Foundation, and a meeting with the mayor and the chairman of the county commission, I was offered the job.

They wanted my decision the next day. I headed home to sleep on it. On my way out of town, I stopped at the Smith's grocery store to buy some snacks for the drive back.

The store was nearly empty, but when I reached the checkout counter, there was a young mother with two small children under the age of three in her shopping cart. They were standing in the cart. Their noses were running, their hair was uncombed and their clothes looked a little dirtier than what should have been. The older one was crying. His mother had swatted him for trying to grab a pack of gum off the impulse-buy display rack.

The woman was already stressed. She was embarrassed because she was having to pull out items that had already been rung up. She didn't have quite enough to pay for it all. As she fished through her purse looking for more food stamps, a stock boy in the back of the store yelled, "He's got a bottle!"

A big, burly miner with a ponytail, wearing a black leather Harley Davidson jacket and heavy mining boots bolted out the front door with the stock boy and store manager in hot pursuit.

After a short chase, they returned with the culprit and brought him to the checkout station. He didn't have a bottle. He had pork chops. It turned out that he was the husband of the woman and the father of the children in front of me in line. He was crying, the young mother was crying, the cashier was crying, and the stock boy was doing his best not to. The store manager, clearly moved by the humiliation of the moment, threw the pork chops into the woman's grocery sack and said, "Here, take them. Just don't do this again."

The enormity of what I was walking into and what I would have to do hit me as I walked out of the store with my purchases. I remember thinking, "If I sign on here, I will be the only person in town whose full-time job it is to fix this."

I took the job. As it turned out, the Greater Grants Industrial Development Foundation office where I worked for the next three years was in an empty strip mall directly across the street from that Smith's store. There were many days that I looked out the window and across the street to that store and relived that family's humiliation.

We eventually attracted a few projects that created a few hundred new jobs, and the community was starting to believe in itself again.

Three years to the month after that emotional scene at the Smiths checkout line, I was in the same store. In fact, I was in the aisle behind the same checkout stand when a middle-aged woman came up to me.

"Are you Mr. Lautman?" she asked.

I said I was.

"Thank you," she said. "You saved my family."

"Really?" I asked.

She told me that her husband had lost his job at one of the uranium mills and had started drinking again. They had exhausted their savings and his unemployment benefits. His truck had been repossessed and they were about to lose their house.

Their two sons, both honor students and star athletes, had begun self-destructing. The younger son's grades had dropped and he had been hanging out with bad kids. The older son had dropped out of high school and had been suspected of doing drugs.

When her husband had got hired at Bagdad Plastics, a company we had recruited to Grants from Arizona, things turned around. He stopped drinking. The family got their truck back and their house payments back on track.

The oldest boy went back to school and was headed to college on a full-ride wrestling scholarship. The younger son had just won top honors in the state science fair.

We were both a little choked up when she finished her story. She waved off my handshake and hugged me for what seemed a little too long in a grocery store aisle. She said she hoped I appreciated how important it was what we were doing.

Her name was Mrs. Griego. Her family, like the family I encountered in that checkout aisle three years earlier, had been nearly destroyed by the contraction of the area's economic base.

That fact that it had all happened—the desperation and humiliation of one stressed out mother three years earlier, and the three-minute hug of gratitude and relief from another—in that same aisle and within sight of my office across the street was surreal.

I realized that this thing we do called economic development had the power to change people's lives and to change communities. If the programs we designed and managed worked, then burly miners wouldn't have to resort to stealing to feed their families.

Families stay together, kids get scholarships and win science fairs instead of dropping out of school and doing drugs.

Those two experiences, more than any others, taught me to pay attention to the good done by our job-creation programs. In Rio Rancho, and later in Santa Teresa, I watched the lives of the families and friends in our neighborhoods improve as they got better jobs and their businesses became more profitable. When our programs work, the character of the community changes for the better, sometimes dramatically.

This more than anything has kept my gumption cycle stoked, albeit sometimes to the point of obsession. I can tell which of my colleagues benchmark their program efforts. Those for whom it is just a job are obvious too.

In the end, I want people to share my conviction that well-conceived and professionally-run economic development efforts can transform economies and communities and profoundly change the lives of people in them.

If more of us do, fewer of our neighbors will have to steal pork chops to feed their families, and more of us will be living in Winnerville.

Conclusion

I think the zero-sum labor market and the looming shortage of qualified labor is our country's number one national security problem. The Inverted Labor Supply Curve will make current standards of living impossible in many communities. It is too serious a risk for prudent people, especially community leaders, to ignore.

In the years running up to the recession, shortages of qualified labor were constraining economies all over the industrialized world. It was especially obvious in rural communities in our region. The Great Recession was only a painful reprieve and a costly distraction. As the economy recovers, we'll be right back facing the same dilemma: jobs, jobs everywhere, but no one qualified to do them.

Children are now viewed as an indulgent luxury by many modern societies—bad for the planet and bad for your career, your balance sheet and the community. For the record, I consider my kids and grandkids to have paid off on sheer entertainment value alone. So have a few more kids. If you raise them right and educate them, it will be good for your community, your country and the planet.

Even then it's going to take a generation or two to get back to where we should be. For the Boomers to fix this we would have to go back thirty years, have four kids and prevent the destruction of our public education system. The damage is done. The results are in. We have to deal with it now. But if there is one thing screaming at us from the population pie chart it's that the two quadrants we need to grow, qualified workers and children, are shrinking, while the two quadrants we need to shrink are exploding. We have no statistical chance of emerging from this with our economy and our values intact if we don't find ways to dramatically shrink the class of unqualified workers and rapidly grow the proportion of qualified workers. The bottom line: We are toast as a country if we don't get the dropout rate down to single digits, realign curriculum with the needs of the future job market and drive up educational achievement.

Catastrophic full employment isn't going to happen in every community, but it has the potential to constrain our national economy enough to make us poorer, weaker, more divided and meaner. There will continue to be high-profile contests between cities and states for headline-making plant locations. But if the Boomers continue to bail, and the schools continue to fail, the majority of U.S. communities will be unable to keep their economies balanced with the service demands of their populations. For these losers, it will feel like perpetual recession. My economic development colleagues and I have three choices: deny, despair or innovate.

For those who choose to innovate our way out, this will be the most exciting time to be in economic development since the profession got started seventy years ago. There are no silver-bullet solutions. But there are things we can do. Some of them are right in front of us, and we should be doing them anyway.

Believe!

And oh yeah, steer clear of the Goat Killers and the CAVE people.

More Reading

Complexity: The Emerging Science at the Edge of Order and Chaos. M. Mitchell Waldrop (1992)

Free Agent Nation: The Future of Working for Yourself, Daniel Pink *(2001)*

Dark Age Ahead, Jane Jacobs (2004)

The New Geography, Joel Kotkin (2002)

The Coming Generational Storm, Laurence Kotlikoff and Scott Burns (2004)

Freakonomics: A Rogue Economist Explores the Hidden Side of Everything, Steven Levitt and Stephen J. Dubner (2005)

Workforce Crisis: How to Beat the Coming Shortage of Skills and Talent, by Ken Dychtwald, Robert Morison, Tamara Erickson (2006)

Hot, Flat, and Crowded: Why We Need a Green Revolution—And How It Can Renew America, Thomas Friedman (2008)

Who's Your City?, Richard Florida (2008)

Outliers, Maclom Gladwell (2008)

Hollowing Out The Middle, Patrick Carr and Maria Kefalas (2009)

What Would Google Do?, Jeff Jarvis (2009)

Shop Class as Soulcraft, Matthew Crawford (2009)

The Age of the Unthinkable, Joshua Cooper Ramo (2009)

INDEX

E

F

G

H

I

J

K

L

M

Mark Lautman has been in the economic development business for three decades. He helped build the economic base for the city of Rio Rancho, New Mexico, in the 1980s, and has designed some of the most successful economic development programs in the country. He is an outspoken critic of the economic development field for its lack of accountability and innovation. He is the founder of Lautman Economic Architecture and the Community Economics Lab in Albuquerque.

Lautman can be reached at: lautman123@gmail.com.